PRAISE FOR
THE AUTHENTICITY CODE™

"All over the world, people are evaluating their very reason for living—rethinking this business of being human, and re-engaging the process of life itself in a new way. This book has perfect timing. Dr. Sharon's new principles show how to find purpose and fulfillment in life. The trick is finding and remaining in touch with these priorities of the heart. That is what *The Authenticity Code*™ is all about."

—**NEALE DONALD WALSCH**, *New York Times* best-selling
author of *Conversations with God*

"If you have ever had doubts about yourself—this book can become your best friend. Dr. Sharon Lamm-Hartman sincerely wants to help you succeed. She wants to help you build your future, enhance your career, and get those promotions/jobs, and financial benefits you know you deserve! The truth is, she has helped thousands make that kind of significant personal progress."

—**MARK VICTOR HANSEN**, #1 *New York Times* best-selling author
and cocreator of the *Chicken Soup for the Soul* Series

"If you want to be absolutely exceptional in your career and job, then this book is a must-read. Authentic Presence can account for more than 80 percent of what it takes to get a job, receive a promotion, or close a deal. Dr. Sharon eloquently teaches her 20+ years of proven material through a moving and inspirational parable of two professionals vying for the same job. The parable keeps your interest all the way through with a surprise ending that is sure to touch every reader's heart. *The Authenticity Code*™—*Your Presence + Your Audience + Your Presentation = Your Success* is so simple yet profound. Cracking the code is the key to having the career of your dreams."

—ALLISON MASLAN, *Wall Street Journal* best-selling author of *Scale or Fail*

"We look for three things in the people we add to our team—and of these three the most important is authenticity because it builds trust with clients, vendors, investors, and customers. Dr. Sharon's book and program provide all the essential traits and tools needed to bring and project one's true self across all those relationships and be truly authentic."

—DAN HART, CEO of Virgin Orbit

"*The Authenticity Code*™ will support you in discovering and using the REAL resonant Power of being your authentic self. Enlightening exercises tied to real-life success stories are woven throughout, guiding you to be able to share your self and your message more impactfully. Practice with the *powerfull* methods in these pages, and receive the miracles in your life."

—SARK, author, artist, inspirationalist, PlanetSARK.com

"Boeing values continuous learning and many of our professionals have seen outstanding growth in their career development through executive presence training. At Boeing, we are committed to being as transparent with our stakeholders as possible and programs like Dr. Sharon's *The Authenticity Code*™ aligns with that commitment, teaching individuals the skills they need to bring the best version of their authentic self forward. It is programs such as this one that are instrumental in developing our current and future generation of leaders."

—**CHRIS RAYMOND, Chief Sustainability Officer and Vice President of Global Enterprise Sustainability, Boeing**

"What an insightful book! Dr. Sharon's formula for authenticity—coupled with her delivery of information through someone else's journey—empowers you to learn, as the characters experience the trials, tribulations, and joys of presenting authentically. After decades of speaking professionally, I can personally attest that the techniques she advocates truly work. And now, I have a couple new tricks up my sleeve. Definitely worth the read!"

—**HEATHER WAGENHALS, columnist, TV talk show host of *Unlock Your Wealth Today*®, member of the National Speakers Association, and ICFE Certified Identity Theft Risk Management Specialist (CITRMS®)**

"No matter how outstanding a student's education is, there is always an area for improvement and that is in presenting themselves authentically. This book gives college students their road map to be successful in the career of their dreams."

—**NORMA CLAYTON, board chair of Tuskegee University**

"If you have a story to tell or an idea to share, the concepts and skills Sharon outlines in this book will show you how to communicate and connect in a clear, genuine, warm, and compelling way. She provides a practical approach to aligning your presence with your message in a way that better serves your audience, the ideas you care about—and your career."

—CRAIG WEBER, best-selling author of *Conversational Capacity* and *Influence in Action*

"I know from both observation and personal experience that if you are serious about career advancement and ongoing success you will need to know and practice two key things. First, know how to present yourself appropriately and professionally to any important 'audience,' whether clients, prospects, or their employers. You need to 'dress and look the part.' Second, know how to present your ideas and goals clearly and convincingly. Learn how to drive your key points home, through organization, word choice, vocal skills, gestures, and movement, as well as the effective use of visual aids and props. I teach presentation skills to all of my clients as it is essential to ensure the greatest success possible and I will make sure they read this book to enhance my training. Dr. Sharon shares very important, strategic, and revealing techniques to improve the effectiveness of your presentation. In short, to reach the height of success, be AUTHENTIC! Dr. Sharon is a widely recognized expert and facilitator who has helped countless players in multiple industries—including those who work in numerous Fortune 500 companies—reach their loftiest goals. The essential elements of her highly successful *AUTHENTIC PRESENCE AND PRESENTATION SKILLS* workshops/seminars not only engage the attendees but also allows them to create more success in their professional careers. Through her desire to impact a larger audience, Dr. Sharon has now made her wisdom and strategies for success available to you and anyone ready to take charge of their future by becoming the best executive by both leading and living authentically. If you want to speed your pathway to greater success and impact, I strongly suggest that you devour every word of this remarkable book. It allows you to crack THE AUTHEN-TICITY CODE™!"

—SHARON LECHTER, CGMA, author of *Think and Grow Rich for Women*, coauthor of *Exit Rich, Outwitting the Devil,* and *Rich Dad, Poor Dad*

THE
AUTHENTICITY
CODE™

THE ART AND SCIENCE OF SUCCESS
AND WHY YOU CAN'T FAKE IT TO MAKE IT

DR. SHARON LAMM-HARTMAN

Creator of APPS: "Authentic Presence and Presentation Skills"

GREENLEAF
BOOK GROUP PRESS

Published by Greenleaf Book Group Press
Austin, TX
www.gbgpress.com

Distributed by Greenleaf Book Group

For ordering information or special discounts for bulk purchases, please contact
Greenleaf Book Group at PO Box 91869, Austin, TX 78709, 512.891.6100.

Design and composition by Greenleaf Book Group and Kimberly Lance
Cover design by Greenleaf Book Group and Kimberly Lance

Publisher's Cataloging-in-Publication data is available.

Print ISBN: 978-1-62634-867-7
eBook ISBN: 978-1-62634-868-4

Part of the Tree Neutral® program, which offsets the number of trees consumed in
the production and printing of this book by taking proactive steps, such as planting
trees in direct proportion to the number of trees used: www.treeneutral.com

THE AUTHENTICITY CODE™ is a trademark of Inside-Out Learning, Inc.

Printed in the United States of America on acid-free paper

20 21 22 23 24 25   10 9 8 7 6 5 4 3 2 1

First Edition

Dedication

To five special groups of people:

My FAMILY, whose unconditional love, patience, and support is the fuel for me taking my work into the world and for completing this book.

My FRIENDS, who helped me laugh on a daily basis and encouraged me to write and publish this book when I wanted to give up.

My TEAMMATES, who always have my back and provided advice, input, and support throughout the process of writing this book.

My CLIENTS who have sponsored, advocated, and believed in this work for the past 20 years, and encouraged me to take this work to a broader audience.

My READERS who are on a quest to becoming even more of their true authentic selves. May this book unlock the code for you to be who you came here to be and do what you came here to do, because our world needs you to be doing this now!

It is to all these wonderful people that I dedicate this book.

Contents

Foreword by Mark Victor Hansen

WE ALL KNOW this to be a fact: There is a right way to do things and a wrong way to do things. The right way will usually bring you success, but the wrong way will often result in failure. This applies in almost every aspect of life . . . especially in your business or career.

If you are asked to speak—to make a presentation to a group of any size or to interview for a new job—there are clearly *right* ways to do it. *Effective* ways! *Memorable* ways!

There are right ways to begin—to draw your audience in and get them hooked.

There are right ways to illustrate your key points—to make them unforgettable and applicable.

There are right ways to end your communication—to issue a significant and meaningful call to action. Perhaps to motivate your audience to "get out there and make a difference," or inspire them to say, "We want you for this position. You're *perfect!*"

There is also a right way to "present yourself." This goes well beyond your material. Your content. Your ideas.

There is a right way to *look*. A right way to dress appropriately for your target audience.

There is a right way to carry yourself. To *stand* and *move*. And maintain eye contact. To be completely professional, to captivate your audience and maintain a solid connection throughout your presentation or interview.

In a formal presentation, there is also a right way to use your charts and slides. Your PowerPoint slides can *entertain*, *inform*, and *persuade*. Or they can confuse your audience and harm your presentation. You simply have to know how to use them in the right way!

This book is about helping you do everything the right way—from the moment you greet your audience to the moment you offer your closing words. It's about what to *say*, what to *do*, how to *look*, and how to *be genuine*. How to be your *authentic self*. Yes, you can be the person others truly respect and to whom they want to pay rapt attention!

The important thing is, if you've ever had doubts about yourself or your ability to capture and hold an audience, this book can become your best friend. Dr. Sharon Lamm-Hartman sincerely wants to help you succeed. She wants to help you build your future, enhance your career, and get those promotions/jobs and financial benefits you *know* you deserve! The truth is, she has helped thousands make that kind of significant personal progress.

If you ignore what Dr. Sharon has to say, you will most likely be impeding your professional advancement.

So, I urge you to read and devour every single word. Commit it all to your memory. Practice it daily.

This book is packed with solid information that has not been "thought up" in order to simply write a book. It has been "thought through" and proven. For those reasons, it works!

I promise you that you will not regret buying this book, reading this book, and learning and applying every single solid tip that it offers. Enjoy!

MARK VICTOR HANSEN

Best-Selling Author and Coauthor of

the *Chicken Soup for the Soul* Series

August 2021

About Mark Victor Hansen

You probably know his name, even if you think you may not. Mark is the creator and coauthor (with Jack Canfield) of the *Chicken Soup for the Soul* series of books—with more than 500,000,000 (half a billion) copies sold according to the *Guinness World Records*. Mark is also the author or coauthor of several other best sellers, including *The Miracles in You, Dare to Win, The Aladdin Factor, The One Minute Millionaire, The Richest Kids in America*, and *Ask!*, coauthored with his wife, Crystal Dwyer Hansen. He is widely recognized as "America's Ambassador of Possibility," as he promotes a "you can do it" attitude to everyone he meets.

Mark is obviously no stranger to the world of writing, publishing, and public speaking/effective presentations. He has, over the years, offered high-powered seminars on these and other topics, and has drawn thousands of attendees who were able and eager to adopt and apply his sound principles of success. He has been paid to speak professionally to millions of people who live in more than 78 countries. He has been given ten honorary doctorates and won the prestigious Horatio Alger Award for Distinguished Americans—those who have lived the proverbial "rags-to-riches" story. Over many years, Mark has also been exceedingly philanthropic.

Currently, Mark and Crystal are immersed in their new venture, designed to bring affordable, renewable energy and innovative devices to the United States—and the world (metamorphosisenergy.us). Watch an informative video at naturalpowerconcepts.com. Their massive transformative purpose is *energy and water independence for everyone, everywhere.*

Acknowledgments

JAMES HARTMAN, MY rock and husband—thank you for always having my back and supporting me, from making me almond milk lattes in the morning to giving me the time and space I needed to write. Thank you for your patience in how long I took to write this book, and for never judging my procrastination habit.

Joshua Hartman, my son and heart—thank you for your patience and support. I know there were many times you wanted me to be spending time with you instead of writing this book. Your letters of support believing in me and what I could create and accomplish helped me believe in myself.

Helen and Dan Lamm, my deceased parents—thank you for having me and being my guardian angels. I miss you each day and feel your presence each day. Thank you for giving me the perseverance, grit, and drive to take my work into the world. Thank you for giving me life so that I could.

Nancy Lamm, my sister, who has always had my back—thank you for believing in me, loving me unconditionally, and helping me laugh. Your support gave me the confidence I needed to finish this book.

Carolyn and Mary Lamm, my sisters, thank you for always being there when I needed you. I am grateful for your love and support.

Thank you to my Inside Out Learning team—Samantha Feuerzeig, Shannon Dodd, Brett Piper, Randy Ganacias, Richard Hodge, Kyndall Abbate, Marsha Petrie-Sue, Phillip Lechter, Mark Spiwak, Marshall Short, Dr. Claire Leon, Dr. Fariba Alamdari, Dr. Diane Shapiro, Jim Meier, Ret. Gen. Craig Cooning, Lisa Ann Landry, and Tom Feltz. Thank you so very much for your unwavering support in encouraging me in taking this work to a broader audience and for believing in the work as much as you do. I also appreciate your input into subtitles, book launch ideas, and so on.

To my clients—such as Chevon Fuller, Mandy Vaughan, Dan Hart, Jesse Harris, Gretchen Wilde, Quentin Blackford, Mike Rokow, Dr. Nancy Shaw, Norma Clayton, and so many more who are just too numerous to name. Thank you so very much for believing in this work, sponsoring programs, and being supportive advocates of knowing and experiencing the powerful transformation that happens in APPS programs.

To friends and colleagues—Elizabeth Catoggio, Dana Sterling, Gretchen Wilde, Craig Weber, Denise Hatch, Dr. Pete Cuozzo, Ann Meredith, Maureen Friel, Trish Baitinger, Marshall Doyle, Jim LaRosa, Mike Breeze, Michelle Adams, Regina Mellinger, Dr. Bradley Williams, Sharon Lechter, Dr. Elaine Ralls, Angela Hallier, Nancy Rhodes and all my WPO sisters—thank you! I could not have done this without your support. There were days I wanted to give up, and your encouragement got me to the finish line. A big thank-you to WBENC Pamela Prince-Eason, Andrew Gaeckle, Laura Taylor, and Pamela Williamson for believing in my work, allowing me to present at WBENC WeThrive, and being so inspired by my work that you bought books for hundreds of WeThrive participants.

To so many of my mentors who saw and believed in my ability to be a thought leader in the professional and leadership development field and who supported me in doing so, including Richard Hodge, SARK,

Dr. Victoria Marsick, Libbi Lepow, Ed Petka, Allison Maslan, Stewart Borie, Dr. Faye Mandell, and all the many others who have helped me be who I am today.

To Steve Gottry, who worked with me to wrap a story around my core APPS research and teachings. Steve was involved in meetings, phone calls, and emails behind this, my essential life's work.

To all who provided testimonials for the book, I am humbled and honored by having your well-known and highly reputable names behind this volume. Thank you for believing in the power of my work.

And most of all, to everyone reading this book—my audience. Without you and your interest, this book would just sit on a shelf in a warehouse somewhere. Thank you for participating in the journey of authentic development with me.

Introduction

HAVE YOU EVER been spellbound?

By that, I mean, have you ever been so drawn in by someone's ideas, communication skills, words, gestures, facial expressions—their *presence*—that you couldn't take your eyes, or ears, off what they were doing right in front of you?

This has happened to me. More than once. In fact, lots of times. I have been wowed by some of the most remarkable, well-known speakers of all time—Zig Ziglar, Brené Brown, General Colin Powell, Madeleine Albright, and many others.

I've also been impressed beyond words by watching and listening to several relatively unknown presenters such as Dr. Fariba Amidari, Jade Simmons, and Akeem Iman-Jones.

On the other hand, I have been in situations where I have had to listen to long, boring, unappealing presentations by some of the worst speakers ever. Completely untrained, uninformed, or unprepared. I felt as though my time had been wasted. (Obviously, I won't call them out by name!)

The fact is, we are always presenting ourselves, whether through formal pitches, informal communications, or interviews for a promotion or an entirely new job.

What is the difference between the outstanding, the good, the bad, and the downright dreadful?

There are so many defining factors that even this book—a book focused on professional presence, presentation, and authenticity—can't bring them all to the forefront. But it *does* offer a solid beginning.

A few of the elements that easily make or break presenters include the following:

- Sincerity: People can easily tell the difference between "fake" and "real."
- Preparation: Always do the homework!
- Content: Is it relevant to the audience and the listener's needs?
- Finishing strong: Is there a clear call to action? Are the decision makers motivated to do something?
- Image and appearance: It's important to look the part.
- "Owning" the environment: Skilled presenters take charge of the room or interview setting.
- Becoming your "authentic brand": This is what earns trust! Again, most people can immediately spot a "fake" or "phony."
- Accepting and dealing with feedback and questions: Does the presenter truly try to meet needs, without getting defensive?

For more than 25 years, I have been focused on helping executives and professionals discover and refine their presence and formal and informal presentation skills. Achieving that end helps them reach desired business results, gain promotions, get the job they need and want, achieve their desired level of personal and professional success, and build unwavering confidence.

Through my company, Inside-Out Learning, Inc. (IOL), my team and I have presented one-hour to five-day versions of my course, Authentic Presence and Presentation Skills (or APPS), to a vast number of Fortune

500 and Inc. 1000 companies, along with small to midsize businesses, nonprofit organizations, and educational institutions. We have also presented virtual and digital modules of our APPS program, and we now have a new app that anyone can use from their cell phones to strengthen their authentic presence and presentation skills. Without exception, the response has been astonishingly positive. The course has propelled participants to unimagined new heights in their careers, sales, and business results, as well as their personal lives. In fact, one of my Fortune 50 clients has offered the training to more than 2,000 key leaders and professionals.

The name of the original program I designed was IOL's Executive Presence and Presentation Skills Program. However, as we interviewed hundreds of program graduates and asked them what they most received from the program, they said, "I connected with the true me, my authentic presence." Many said that before the program, they tried to be someone they were not, and were trying to "fake it to make it." During the program they found confidence in who they truly are as a leader or professional, as well as who they are becoming. They also became more service-minded and realized they must interact with their audience and tailor their message and presence to their audience in order to be of maximum service to their listeners. The Authenticity Code™ helped them unravel the art and science of success.

Of course, you may be asking, "How can you prove your claims?"

I believe that the proof is evident in four measures:

1. **How do participants evaluate the course when it is over?** Our average score across thousands of participants on a scale of 1 to 5, with 5 being exceptional, is 4.9. Most program participants say that the program is the "best they have ever taken."

2. **How successful are our participants over the long term after they have gone through the training?** About 50 to 80 percent of participants are promoted or land their ideal job within one year of attending the program, and many say they could not have achieved that promotion without applying what they learned in the program. Companies also experience a 90 percent retention rate of participants who go through our three- and five-day programs. The participants feel motivated, inspired, and valued—which encourages them to stay with the company. Our entrepreneur participants take their companies to a completely new level of success and build their ideal teams.

3. **How many clients sign up to repeat the training and invite other team members—or recommend the course to other associates?** We have a long wait list of people who want to go through our program because program graduates nominate so many.

4. **How much more money does our program help our participants make?** Our clients have experienced billions of dollars in sales from presentations that our participants develop in the program. Participants work on actual presentations and get detailed feedback and coaching on them, and they go out and use these presentations to make direct sales for their company. Increased sales and revenue is an outcome for both our Fortune 500 participants and small to midsize business CEOs and teams.

And here is a bonus measure:

5. **Participants say that it helps them "get to yes" faster in any communication they make, whether the communication is for an internal or external audience.** Participants affirm that their influence, communication, and leadership skills improve dramatically.

My underlying reason for writing this book is not to convince you that I have built an effective program. Rather, my purpose is to empower and inspire those readers who, for whatever reason, can't attend the course. My goal is to provide you with both the encouragement and the tools to become a more effective communicator—and to let your authenticity and your skills speak *for* you. This book will give you a personal road map to the art and science of your success. I am chasing that objective through what I hope you will find to be an engaging story (or "parable") packed with simple truths that anyone can apply—and that you can benefit from immediately.

This book addresses some important cutting-edge questions such as: what if instead of thinking authenticity is all about you, you thought of it as being about you and others? What if you could turn your greatest wound into your greatest authentic gift to give? What if instead of thinking of authenticity as a trait like integrity, we reimagined it as a skill that we can learn to become more authentic?

I call this book *The Authenticity Code*™, because, in the case of in-person and virtual communications, those who fake it will never make it. Success in any endeavor demands authenticity, and breaking the code requires this formula: Your Presence + Your Audience + Your Presentation = Your Success.

I describe "authenticity" as "your most powerful way of adding value by expressing your unique gifts and talents for your chosen audience."

Join me on this easy-to-follow journey as I decode the art and science of success with you and for you! My sole goal is to empower you to become your authentic self and achieve your desired level of success.

I hope you enjoy this fun, engaging, and honest parable as a roadmap to the journey of becoming more authentic and achieving what you most want both personally and professionally. At the end of many (but not all) of the chapters in this book, I will give you an opportunity to briefly apply what you learned in the chapter to your own life and career.

1

Chasing the Same Dream

EVEN THOUGH THEY worked for the same company, World Wide Synergistics, in essentially the same department—Sales and Marketing—Rachel Hannigan and Joshua Armstrong were very different in many ways. Yet at the same time, they were also similar in several other ways. They both wanted the promotion to associate director of Sales. As one might expect, their talents and abilities were unique and diverse.

It was no secret to anyone in the company that Rachel and Joshua were very competitive. Fortunately, they also played fair so that their ambitions did not diminish their ethics or integrity. Rachel was the more transparent of the two. Josh tended to be more protective of his thought processes, his goals, and his career objectives. And even his accomplishments.

They both knew that a long, arduous interview process was ahead of them. World Wide Synergistics did not take these promotions lightly. There were mandatory hoops to jump through.

Management correctly surmised that the decision they faced would be a difficult one. Rachel and Josh knew their stuff. They understood the basics of sales and marketing—and beyond. On top of that, they had both graduated with honors from highly respected universities and had eagerly—but patiently—honed their skills on the job. Rachel had become the go-to person on social media and internet presence. Josh had found his home in writing clear and concise marketing materials and easy-to-follow operating manuals for the company's entire product line. He knew how to turn "tech speak" into plain English . . . and plain Spanish, French, German, and Russian. (Josh might have been one of the more multi-fluent linguists on earth!)

Yes, it would be a difficult choice. What, if anything, would separate the two candidates? As you may have already guessed, that factor would be authenticity or, more specifically, *authentic presence*. The one who could crack The Authenticity Code™ the most clearly and convincingly would gain the promotion. But I am getting a bit ahead of myself. Of course, there is much more to this story.

TAKE A MOMENT . . .

1. In your career, what position or promotion would you truly value right now?

_____

_____

2. If you could choose any job in any field and in any company, what would it be?

_____

_____

3. How do you define success both personally and professionally? What does it look like for you?

_____

_____

I remember when I realized I wanted to be CEO of my own company, and I was still working for a Fortune 500 company. Around the same time, I wrote down my personal and professional definition of success. In addition to running a successful business, I wanted to be personally healthy, be part of a healthy family, live in a home I truly felt at home in, move to a place with lots of sunshine and warmth, have close friendships and a supportive community, be spiritually connected, and to feel I made a difference in the world. The first step in helping you achieve your desired level of success is to name it. And the next step is to crack *The Authenticity Code*™. I know this because not only have I helped thousands of students, professionals and leaders achieve their desired level of success by cracking *The Authenticity Code*™, but I also walk my talk and I can say this worked for me. I want to help you do the same, so let's continue.

2

The First "Battle Round"

FOR MANY SEASONS, millions of TV viewers have watched *The Voice*, a singing competition. In the course of the season, two performers are paired for a "battle round." They compete against each other and the judges decide who wins the battle. The winners of the battles advance to the next round of competition.

Rachel and Josh were about to face their first "battle round." Their main judge would be Ron Burk, VP of Sales. His decision would be final, although he had the option of including Victoria Reynolds, VP of Human Resources, in the decision-making process. To his credit, Ron had made universally accepted promotion decisions in the past.

Ron called Rachel and Josh to his office, which was step one of the decision process.

Ron sat back in his chair and took a good look at the two of them. "I want you both to prepare a presentation that will convince me why I should choose you for this important position," he said. "You have the freedom to do any kind of presentation you'd like, so long as you limit your pitch to 15 minutes."

Rachel nodded and said, "Sounds like a fun challenge."

Josh didn't make effective eye contact with Ron—something Ron immediately noticed. Josh also said absolutely nothing, but in his mind were these words: *Yes, this definitely is a challenge, but "fun" is not a word I'd use to describe it.*

"Okay," Ron said. "We meet in Conference Room 101 this Friday at 11:00 a.m."

When the meeting ended, Rachel and Josh went back to their work spaces. (One of the perks of this promotion was that the "winner" would leave her or his cramped desk in a huge, wall-less, wide-open work area and move into an office with walls and a door. With an administrative assistant! That certainly appealed to them both.)

Preparation is the key, Rachel thought.

Preparation is the key, Josh thought.

I hope they have both figured out that preparation is essential, Ron thought.

Rachel and Josh took similar steps to prepare for their presentations.

Both of them updated and printed their résumés. As each of them prepared their presentation, they made an effort to point out their "quality educations" and their stellar GPAs.

Rachel decided to make a big deal out of the fact that she had— almost single-handedly—more than *quadrupled* the number of followers the company had on social media. She'd done this all while volunteering significant chunks of time to her charity of choice, the Leukemia and Lymphoma Society. She had discovered this organization through her sorority at college . . . and she stayed with it after graduation. (It had personal meaning for her because her best friend and a sorority sister in college had battled leukemia.)

Josh chose to point out that his clearly worded user manuals were nearly universally praised by customers and competitors alike. Josh included one of his customer's testimonials on his résumé—"Thanks to your manuals, I know what your products are supposed to do, and I understand how to use them." Josh also planned to mention that his astute media buys for the company had saved World Wide Synergistics hundreds of thousands of dollars over the past two years. He chose to sell himself with these words: "I know how to precisely determine what our primary target customers are reading and watching. So I never have to waste money on the unlikely 'possibilities' in the fringe markets. *And* I know how to communicate with them clearly."

Rachel and Josh both made careful and complete notes, and prepared photocopies of their records of individual achievements.

I'm prepared, they both decided.

TAKE A MOMENT . . .

1. How would you describe your relationship with your boss or immediate supervisor? If you are looking for a job, describe the relationship you would like to have with your boss.

   _____

   _____

2. If you are a boss, how would you describe your relationship with your team? If you don't yet have a team, describe the team you would like to have.

   _____

   _____

3. In what ways do you think you could improve the relationships you described in the previous questions?

   _____

   _____

3

So Much for Preparation . . .

THE BIG DAY arrived, much sooner than either Rachel or Josh had anticipated. It was Friday at 11:00 a.m., and they entered Conference Room 101. But it was now or never.

Josh presented first. He mistakenly thought this was "casual Friday," so he wore a clearly pressed pair of dress jeans, accompanied by a "We Don't Need Your Permission" football slogan T-shirt from his alma mater, Vanderbilt University. (Ron had no clue what that meant!) Josh's athletic sneakers were scuffed and dirty . . . and looked as though they had most recently seen the rugby field at college. The most upscale thing about his appearance was his fancy watch—a costly Breitling titanium Aerospace model that somehow didn't seem out of place on his wrist.

His entire presentation took him less than eight minutes, even though he had clearly been allotted 15 minutes. No wasted words. That made Ron wonder if Josh somehow missed some key points he might have presented.

Rachel was the opposite in many ways but also thought it was "casual Friday." She was dressed in what many in the professional world would consider to be a hippie look. She wore sandals that looked like they were from the 1960s, along with jeans that had those trendy frayed rips in them.

In an effort to make sure she used every minute available to make her case, Rachel took the 15 minutes allotted to her. Then 20 minutes. Then 26:35. (Ron thought, *Time to sit down, Rachel. We know you want the promotion, and you are trying really hard to connect with me with all your personal stories. No mistaking that!*)

Ron's other thoughts at the time were mixed. *I thought they would both be more effective than they were. As the associate director of Sales, they'll always be presenting—whether formally, informally, or while wining and dining with customers. Perhaps I selected the wrong two candidates. There are plenty of good people in this company.*

But immediately following their presentations, Ron was silent for a minute or two. Then he asked a question: "Do you recall when we offered The Authenticity Code™: Authentic Presence and Presentation Skills— APPS—course as a benefit to our employees? The last time we offered it was about a month ago."

Atypically, Josh responded first. "I remember hearing about it. But I was in Philadelphia at a convention that entire week. Can't be in two places at the same time."

Rachel chirped: "I recall hearing about it, but I had no idea what APPS even is."

Ron tried to conceal his shock that neither candidate had participated in this special gift to the company's employees. *That's obviously why both of their presentations were weak*, he thought.

"APPS is a program for people with professional advancement or leadership potential," Ron continued. "It helps you to crack The Authenticity Code™, which is Your Presence + Your Audience + Your Presentation = Your Success. It is generally offered as a virtual or live training course that has also been presented to numerous Fortune 500 companies and other organizations, including Virgin Orbit, Boeing, Equistar Chemicals LP, WBENC, Dexcom, Airpark Signs and Graphics, VOX Space, and some government agencies and universities to name a few. It's also offered publicly, so if you can't make one of our company-sponsored dates, you can sign up for a public course on Inside-Out Learning's website."

"Quite an impressive list of companies," Rachel observed.

"Yes, it really is," Ron agreed. "And that's why we decided to offer it to our forward-moving team members so that you'll 'be all you can be,' to borrow a recruiting phrase from the US Army. It is a remarkable, proven program that brings out your authentic gifts and talents in a way that works for your audience and helps you deliver exceptional formal and informal presentations.

"I have to be completely honest," Ron continued. "Right now, if it came down to this being between the two of you for this vital position, I'd have to choose 'none of the above.'"

Both candidates looked as if Ron had just splashed them with ice-cold water, their eyes widening in shock.

Finally, Rachel mustered enough boldness to ask, "Why, Ron?"

Ron thought for a moment. "So many possible answers . . . so little time to tell you."

More stunned expressions from Rachel and Josh.

But, despite his somewhat brutal candor, Ron had a heart.

"Tell you what. If you really want some help from a relatively long-time employee who has really been through it all, I would be happy to help you. I have been where you are right now."

"I'd be interested," they said in unison.

"Good! Here's the thing. We would meet for an hour once a week for me to mentor you on developing your authentic presence and presentation skills. Can you make time for that? This will change your lives *and* your future. I promise."

"I'm in," Rachel replied.

Josh said, "I guess I'll do it."

"Great! See you next Monday morning at nine. Please bring a notebook with lots of pages. You may also use your cell phone, laptop, or iPad. Just so long as you can take detailed notes. I am serious!"

"Got it. Monday morning at nine. Bring notebook, computer, phone, or tablet. I'll be here!" Rachel said.

Josh replied, "I'll be here, too!"

4

Ron Becomes "Mr. Mentor"

THE FOLLOWING MONDAY, both Rachel and Josh showed up at Ron's office at precisely 8:57 a.m. They were both so eager and excited they nearly collided in the hallway. A big promotion sure was enticing bait!

They settled into the comfortable overstuffed leather chairs in Ron's office.

I'm ready, Rachel thought. She couldn't have been more disappointed in herself for not meeting Ron's expectations last Friday. Being the perfectionist she was, she'd beaten herself up with negative self-talk all weekend. She planned to dedicate herself to cracking The Authenticity Code™ and developing her authentic presence and presentation skills so she could land the associate director of Sales job that she so desperately wanted.

I could fall asleep watching football in this great chair, Josh thought. *But I'll try to stay awake. I really want this! I think.* Josh had tried to put this out of his mind all weekend and focused on the latest tech invention he was designing. Even with trying to put it out of his mind, he did start to doubt himself, wondering whether he really was the best candidate for this position.

As some wise person once observed, "Motivation really *does* spring from desire." (And maybe from need, too.)

"So, you're probably wondering why I called this meeting," Ron opened, striving for a bit of humor.

Rachel and Josh nodded affirmatively.

"I was kidding. I simply want to help you both. Not just for this promotion, but for your long-term career and life success as well."

"Thank you!" Rachel and Josh said in unison.

"Okay, here are my thoughts on your presentations. Rachel, you ran long. That's because you added too much unnecessary detail. Too much detail loses your audience. You also shared a lot of personal stories, when I was looking more to get down to business. Josh, your presentation ran short. *Way* short. Another thing: Too little detail without enough relevant information will not get a yes from your audience. The ultimate goal of any presentation is to get key people to buy into your pitch. To get them to accept and help promote your goals . . . and likely even financially support them."

Both employees nodded.

"Well, no matter if you ran short or long, what was really missing from both of your pitches were two basic things—authentic presence and presentation skills. I hate to be so blunt, but your content was weak and poorly organized, and your presentations did not hold my interest."

They both had puzzled looks on their faces.

Ron continued: "If either of you get this promotion, along with other possible promotions that might follow, you will likely be making presentations to the C-suite of our company, as well as our customers' companies. These are the people whose titles begin with the letter C. Chief financial officer. Chief operating officer. Chief marketing officer. Chief of research and development. Yes, and even our chief executive officer . . . our CEO."

"Got it," Josh responded flippantly.

"Thank you," Rachel said with sincerity.

Ron got them back on track. "I'm really sorry that neither one of you participated in the APPS training. Of course, it was a free *optional* benefit, but I highly recommend you sign up for, at a minimum, the digital version of the program. The course will help you crack and apply The Authenticity Code™ in your careers. At its core, the code means learning how to combine essential professional and leadership components that will lead to the result you want: Your Presence + Your Audience + Your Presentation = Your Success.

"But even though you haven't taken the APPS program, I still feel compelled to help you both as much as I possibly can, by offering the basics in our upcoming meetings. I selected you both. I want one of you to succeed in the short term . . . and both of you over the long term."

"We appreciate your commitment," Rachel offered.

"Yeah," Josh chimed in.

"You're most welcome," Ron responded. "And there's no time like the present to get started! We have 45 minutes of our hour remaining, so I'd like to begin to tell you about the first of five keys to successful presentations."

Rachel took out her notepad.

Josh yawned and muttered, "Okay."

Ron mentally recorded both responses.

"Here's the thing," Ron began, "there are several vital keys to making an effective presentation. There are also a number of keys to establishing your 'authentic presence' and tailoring your message to 'your audience.' It is those crucial factors that make you more professional and believable and give you indisputable authenticity.

"Today, and during the sessions that will follow, we'll be discussing making effective presentations and combining those ideas with how to maximize your authentic presence. It takes both your presence plus your presentation to deliver a memorable and meaningful message to your audience. As you know, there are several different kinds of presentations—telephone meetings, video conferences, virtual meetings, live events, written presentations, and, of course, even job interviews where you are presenting yourself and your credentials. We won't be discussing written presentations in our meetings, because it is an incredibly involved and specialized area. Ideally, your writing skills would be stellar, and, as you know, the written word can be extremely persuasive. The downside is that you don't get the immediate feedback you would normally get from the other methods. And, as it has long been said, 'Feedback is the breakfast of champions!' Feedback helps you refine your content, as well as sharpen your presentation skills."

"I *love* feedback!" Rachel said enthusiastically.

"I hate it," Josh responded in a sullen fashion. "I don't think it's ever helped me one bit."

"Josh, you might change your mind as time goes on," Ron suggested.

TAKE A MOMENT . . .

1. A mentor is someone you really admire who is where you would like to be someday. Who are your mentors? If you don't have one, who could you ask to mentor you?

_____

_____

2. In what ways has feedback from others helped you?

_____

_____

5

Know Your Audience:
The First Step to Effectiveness

RON RESUMED THE session without delay. "In order to deliver the most effective presentation you possibly can," he said, "it's vital that you know as much about your audience as you can possibly ascertain.

"The more you know about your audience—especially the key decision maker(s)—the better your presentation will likely go. This is why 'your audience' is an integral part of The Authenticity Code™: Your Presence + *Your Audience* + Your Presentation = Your Success."

"That makes sense to me," Rachel commented.

"Yeah," Josh added.

"Okay, when it comes to your possible promotion, who is your audience? Who is the key decision maker?"

"You are," they both immediately suggested.

"Very good! You've got the picture. But what do either of you really know about me?"

Ron was met with a deafening silence that seemed to go on forever.

"Well . . . I'm waiting. Any thoughts?"

Rachel thought she'd give it a shot. "Well, I know that you have been with World Wide Synergistics longer than both of us have. And I know that you have been promoted twice and that you once held the position both of us are after. So that means the position we want has the potential of leading to even greater things. After all, you are a VP."

"Good so far," Ron observed. "But do either of you know anything about my background? About what I did for years before I was hired here? And what I want for my future?"

"Nope," Josh admitted.

"No clue at all," Rachel concurred.

Ron decided to let them off the hook. "Part of the reason could be because you have never seen or read my 'Authentic Brand Statement.' And that could well be because I have never shared it with anyone in the company."

"Um . . . your *what*? I've never heard of that," Rachel confessed.

Ron finally cracked a smile. "Before I joined World Wide Synergistics, I was a lieutenant colonel in the United States Air Force. That was my first career. My Air Force experience made me of interest to World Wide Synergistics."

Josh was suddenly emboldened. "So that might explain your aversion to both shorter and longer presentations? Your days started at six a.m. sharp and ended at ten p.m. sharp? Right? Time was important? Everything was by the book?"

Rachel glared at Josh, as if she were saying, "You'd better cool it, dude."

However, Ron actually laughed. "Yes, completely by the book, as you said. But it was much more than that. I had to present myself authentically to my superior officers. I had to dress the part and *be* the person I wanted to be. When I signed up for the air force, I was basically choosing my audience for years, for decades. When I joined World Wide Synergistics, I was again choosing my audience. Dressy and formal. No scuffs on my shoes, or T-shirts or frayed jeans." Rachel and Josh looked a bit uneasy, as they obviously knew he was referring to the way they were dressed for their presentation. "Instead I chose tailored pants, dress shirts, and sometimes suit jackets. Why? Because at World Wide Synergistics we deal with customers who are the military and other large formal corporations. Unless you are a 'casual icon' like Richard Branson—whom I greatly admire, of course—you need to dress for your audience. You want your audience to hear your message, and not be focused on what you are wearing because it is so different from what they wear. Heck, when I came here, one executive wore scuffed shoes when presenting to a military audience with five generals. After the presentation, one of the generals came up to my boss and said he did not hear one thing the executive said because he could not get past looking at his shoes."

Rachel and Josh started to giggle almost uncontrollably.

"Sorry," Rachel quickly confessed. "I didn't mean to laugh. But seriously they got hung up on his shoes? That's unbelievable!"

Ron was still smiling. "The truth is, I don't recall anyone who signed up for the military who did not wear pressed clothes with freshly shined shoes. The executive lost his audience because of shoes. Again, this is the importance of knowing your audience."

"Here's the thing. Let's say that someone gets hired to play the part of a character at Disneyland or Walt Disney World. They want to appear as Moana or even Aladdin or Mickey Mouse."

"That would be fun, I think," Rachel thought aloud.

"Could be," Ron agreed. "Here's the point, though. If you want to work in a Disney park, you are deliberately choosing your audience. Kids. Families. So, Disney management used to prohibit visible tattoos while employees were working. Recently they changed their policy to allow cast members to show 'appropriate' visible tattoos, yet they still ask that employees choose hair colors that look natural. They ask their employees to think Disney with every move. Like would Aladdin chew gum while flying on his magic carpet?.

"If you want to work for World Wide Synergistics, you have to adapt to the audiences you will face here because you are choosing your audiences by choosing to work here. Of course, this means dressing, speaking, and acting in ways that are consistent with who we are as a company and as a culture. If you did not authentically fit with our culture and internal and external audiences, you would have chosen a different company with different audiences. We also have a key responsibility to create a workplace culture where people feel welcomed, valued, and respected.

Rachel and Josh were both trying to take in what Ron was saying, but they were both having trouble with the concept of needing to dress the part. Rachel thought to herself—"isn't that inauthentic?" She decided to wait until another time to ask that question.

"As part of our weekly meetings, I will sometimes be giving you handouts. Here is the handout package for what I'm sharing with you today. To continue with 'knowing your audience,' turn to pages three and four in your handouts: There you will see the questions you should always ask yourself before every presentation."

Rachel and Josh flipped through the pages. This was what they saw:

KEY QUESTIONS TO ASK YOURSELF AND OTHERS:

- WHO MATTERS THE MOST AND WHY?

- HOW DOES THAT PERSON MAKE DECISIONS?
  Facts? Emotions? Personality type?

- DOES THIS PERSON SEEM TO HAVE A LOT OF LOYAL FOLLOWERS?
  If so, who are they?

  When possible, conduct a pre-briefing with the main decision maker (or if that is not possible, pre-brief at least one of their loyal followers) to help set up the presentation for success.

"Answering these questions about your key decision makers is the best way to proceed from this point forward," Ron offered.

"This makes sense to me," Rachel replied.

"Great!" Ron continued. "First, ask yourself, 'Who is the leader? How do I know? Why do I believe that?'"

Rachel responded, "Those are good questions to ask."

Josh nodded in agreement.

"Next, what is the background of the primary person you are presenting to? Are they the senior leader? If so, they probably like the 'bottom line up front,' often referred to as 'BLUF.' That simply means, what are the key takeaways on whatever they need to know? If you don't know, find and ask key followers who do know.

"Do you understand how to translate your key points into appropriate language so the decision maker clearly understands them?"

Ron knew he'd been on a roll. This was important to him . . . and to Rachel and Josh, too.

"The next obvious step is to determine who the key followers are.

"For example, to whom does the leader listen, and who are the people seated closest to the leader? Do you think that these key followers may seek different or additional information from your presentation so that they can influence the leader?

"Ultimately, there are four key questions you must ask of yourself and others who know the audience you are presenting to, prior to even beginning to write the presentation. Otherwise, you are writing the presentation for yourself instead of your audience. It is a mistake to just start writing a presentation and never put yourself in your audience's shoes.

"These four key questions will help your presentations and general communication advance from average to exceptional. The four questions are known as the 'audience-understanding matrix.'

"First, what is <u>most important</u> to them?

"Second, what <u>specific details</u> do they need?

"Third, what will <u>hook them</u> to listen to you?

"Finally, where are they willing to <u>compromise</u>? By that, I mean, what are they willing to trade out—such as cost, quality, or schedule—in order to reach the best possible outcome?

"These questions are helpful to ask about your audience prior to starting to write a formal presentation, as well as in general meetings, communications, and job interviews. Let's say that you are interviewing for a promotion, as you are in this case, or you are seeking a new position with another company. You are, in fact, making a presentation. So, you will want to ask those four questions to learn more about your audience, and you will want to speak in your audience's language. After all, this was an authentic choice for you to be in front of that audience, so you are there to be of service to them."

Rachel said, "I never thought about it that way, Ron. I always just start writing a presentation or preparing notes for a meeting or job interview before putting myself in the audience's shoes. Thank you for this important insight."

"Yes, thank you," Josh agreed.

Again, Ron was happy with their responses. "As you might guess, there is another long-established way to identify and utilize the personality characteristics of the key decision makers—those people in your audience with whom you most clearly and convincingly communicate. There are several personality assessments on the market, DISC, Myers-Briggs Type Indicator (MBTI), Insights, and Birkman, just to name a few. In fact, Inside-Out Learning uses some of these assessments in its longer in-person programs. What I love about IOL's shorter virtual and in-person APPS course is that IOL has its own assessment that is super easy to use. It is called the Style Recognition Assessment. Not only does it have four personality styles, but it also gives you clues for how to analyze what style your key audience members are, as well as how to adapt your communication to influence that style of audience. It is brilliant!

"Without me going into all the details offered in the APPS course, the two graphics I am handing to you show the basic descriptions of IOL's four style recognition preferences and clues for recognizing each.

STYLE RECOGNITION—FOUR STYLE PREFERENCES

	PEOPLE PEOPLE	PARTY PEOPLE	PLANNER PEOPLE	POINT PEOPLE
Pattern	Open/Indirect	Open/Direct	Guarded/Indirect	Guarded/Direct
Pace & Orientation	Slower/People Oriented	Faster/People Oriented	Slower/Task Oriented	Faster/Task Oriented
Their Goal	Steadiness	Influencing Others	Compliance	Dominance
Work Area	Casual, Conforming	Stylish, Interesting	Formal, Functional	Busy, Structured
Wants to	Build & Maintain Relationships	Interact & Be Recognized	Gather Information & Know Process	Get to the Bottom Line & Decide Quickly
Fear	Conflict	Loss of Prestige	Embarrassment	Loss of Control
Aggravated by	Insensitivity	Routine	Surprises	Indecision
Makes Decisions by	Considering Options	Spontaneity	Deliberate Action	Decisiveness
Decisions Are	Careful	Impulsive	Planned	Steadfast
Measures Success by	Compatibility, Depth of Relationships	Recognition, Applause, Compliments	Precision, Accuracy, Activity	Results, Track Record, Progress

STYLE RECOGNITION – VERBAL CLUES

Listen carefully in a virtual setting to the words used.

SPEED-READ PEOPLE – READING OTHERS' STYLES

Verbal Clues: If you meet someone, especially for the first time, and they come on strong, they are likely either a **Party or Point Person**.

If they are quiet and soft-spoken, they are probably a **People** or **Planner Person**.

NEXT CLUES: WHAT THEY SAY

STYLE	TYPICAL STATEMENTS	
Point Person	"Tell him I want to talk to him ASAP!" "Let's get this settled right now!" "What's the bottom line?" "Cut to the chase; what are the options?"	"Here's how we'll proceed . . ." "I want to win this—no ifs, ands, or buts." "Tell me what the goal is." "You handle it, but keep me informed."
Party Person	"Hey! Here's an idea! Whattaya think?" "Why don't you noodle on that for a while?" "I feel this is the way we ought to go." "Tell me what you think about . . ."	"Spare me the details. Just give me the drift." "I think we're making progress. Now let's . . ." "My sense is that . . ." "Let's try it a different way, just for kicks."
People Person	"I'd like to go kind of slow on this. Is that okay?" "Have we determined the impact of this on the staff?" "I really enjoy working with you." "I'd like to help you however I can."	"We can work this out, I'm sure." "How do you really feel about this?" "How's this likely to end up? I'd like to know first."
Planner Person	"Now, let's look at this logically." "Is that really the right thing to do? Can we justify that?" "Let's take this first step. Then we can decide step two." "Give me all the facts first."	"What guidelines make sense for this project?" "Precisely what do you mean?" "I don't want any surprises." "Have we touched all the bases?"

"It's vital that we all realize that there is no 'right' or 'wrong' or 'better' or 'worse' style. We are all different. The main reason this is significant is that the people to whom you present all make decisions in different ways. Understanding what is important to them is a critical component for effective communication. If your decision maker is a point person and you are a people person—and you don't present according to their 'get to the point' preferences—you will completely lose your decision maker and, worse yet, frustrate them. The opposite also applies.

"IOL's experience demonstrates that the majority of senior executive decision makers who listen to your presentation are most likely to fall in one of the four personality styles—which is the point person.

"What we know about point people is that they are primarily personality styles who prefer BLUF (bottom line up front), an orderly presentation flow, and a clear, concise presentation. They are often, but not always, the C-suite executives within your company. They are busy and face a lot of time pressure."

After they had all finished reading, Josh asked one of the most significant questions he had posed to this point.

Josh asked Ron, "Okay, so which one are you? After all, you are the audience for our presentations. While we're at it, which one am I? And what is Rachel, my competitor for the promotion?"

"Great questions! Very perceptive!" Ron paused for a moment to consider his full response.

"Before I answer that question, Josh, as I shared, IOL's experience shows that many C-suite executives tend to be point people, but not all. This is consistent with the 2014 *Myers-Briggs Manual*, where the most prevalent four types among executives and senior managers are stated to be ISTJ (20.7 percent), ESTJ (22.8 percent), INTJ (11.2 percent), and ENTJ (17.7 percent). All together, these four MBTI types account for

31

72.4 percent of all executives. And these four types share the MBTI dimensions of TJ, otherwise known as thinking-judging. This correlates very closely to IOL's point people. As I said, get-to-the-point styles prefer bottom line up front: brief, clear, and to-the-point communication. Now, don't get me wrong; I know plenty of successful executives who are different personality styles, like my air force buddy General Al Scinto, CEO of ISSI, who is a planner person, and my wife, who is a people person and chief technology officer for a major government agency.

"Instead of just telling you what style I am, I would rather you use IOL's style recognition clues document to guess what I am based on clues I have given you." (See chart on page 30.)

Josh interjected, "I think I know what you are because of many clues you have given us, and my absolute favorite board game ever is CLUE. I seldom lose that game."

Ron smiled and laughed with approval. "Go for it, Josh!"

"Okay, based on my limited understanding of you so far, you have gotten down to business quickly in our meetings; you want one of us to win this promotion; and you told Rachel she spoke too long in her initial presentation. So all of these clues lead me to believe that you are a point person. Your military background would suggest to me that you can make fast decisions more from a logical perspective—and you seem to like organization, decisions, and plans over spontaneity. Again, all of these clues suggest you have a personality preference of being a point person."

"I'm impressed, Josh. You nailed it!"

Ron continued: "When you enroll in the APPS, you will learn more about how to present to each of the four different types. You can give the same presentation in four different ways based on who the key decision maker in the audience is."

Rachel said, "Wait, I also see that you care deeply about us because you are taking your personal time to help us. You are very giving of your time, and you are mentoring us. You also told Josh he ran too short. So that would suggest to me that you are a people person."

Ron smiled. "Rachel, that is a brilliant observation. We are not just one of these four types; we have a preferred style that we lead from, and we also have a secondary style, and we may even have characteristics in several of these types. My secondary style is that of a people person. I do care deeply about people, and my main preference is that which I make decisions from, and that is as a point person. Now Josh, in his initial presentation, went too much to the point, so I was not clear on some of the points he was making. In the APPS program, you can take the IOL style recognition assessment to see what your main preference is, and I consistently test as a point person.

"I believe you, Rachel, are a people person because, in your initial presentation, you spent a lot of time connecting with the audience by sharing a lot of personal stories. You also volunteer your time at the Leukemia and Lymphoma Society, which I think is terrific. I will give you one hint: As a point person, I don't want to take time to connect in a presentation. Instead, I want to get to the point quickly, keep relationships businesslike, and use facts—not personal feelings. I also like being precise, effective, and well organized. I love hearing about competitive results and growth opportunities and recommending alternative actions with brief supporting analyses. If we speak our own language to a key decision maker who has a different preferred language, we lose them."

"But isn't that being inauthentic?" Rachel asked.

Ron shared, "Rachel, are you choosing to go for this job? Are you choosing to work in this company? Are you choosing to participate in this mentoring program with me to get this job? Are you choosing to present to me as your audience and the hiring leader?"

"Yes, Ron, you are correct. I think what you are saying is I am authentically choosing you as my audience, so I need to be me and at the same time tailor my message to your preferred style."

"You got it, Rachel. I admire and accept your 'people' nature, and it is what makes you a great sales professional because you can easily feel what others are feeling. There is often a misperception that authenticity is only about being you, with total disregard for your audience. The truth is we choose the audiences we want to be in front of by choosing our employer and career path. We need to also be in service to those audiences. This is where servant leadership intersects with authenticity."

"Thank you for sharing this, Ron," Rachel said. "Now we know how to speak your language in our final presentation, and to be honest, I never thought about any of this before."

"You got the point, Rachel. Great job. Josh, you also asked what style you are. I highly encourage both you and Rachel to go to insideoutlearning.com/style/ and take their style recognition assessment so you can each confirm what your preferred style is."

TAKE A MOMENT . . .

1. Who, most likely, will be in the audience for your next formal or informal presentation? Who is the key decision maker?

_____

_____

_____

_____

2. What do you already know about them? Try answering the four questions on the audience-understanding matrix posed in this chapter: (1) What is <u>most important</u> to them? (2) What <u>specific details</u> do they need? (3) What will <u>hook them</u> to listen to you? And (4) where are they willing to <u>compromise (cost, quality, schedule, safety)</u>?

_____

_____

_____

_____

3. Do you know your preferred personality style of the four described on page 29, and if so, what is it? If not, you receive one complimentary style recognition assessment as a thank-you for purchasing this book, and you can take your assessment by going to insideoutlearning.com/style/.

_____

_____

_____

_____

4. By observing your key decision maker(s) behaviors, look for the clues (shared on page 30) for what personality style they prefer. Write down the clues you see in the decision maker(s) you currently present to and communicate with.

_____

_____

_____

_____

_____

6

Know Yourself: The First Step Toward Authenticity

OR THE FIRST time in their three-way meeting, Josh found himself becoming more involved and showing some genuine interest in what was going on around him.

"You said a moment ago that we have never seen or read your Authentic Brand Statement because you have never shared it with anyone in the company. Would you be willing to share it with us now?" Josh asked.

"I sure would," Ron agreed. "In fact, it's on page five of the handout packet I gave you."

In unison, they flipped pages until they got to page five.

RON BURK'S AUTHENTIC BRAND STATEMENT:

I am the CEO of World Wide Synergistics (#1) who seeks out and hires the most competent, skilled, innovative individuals I can identify for every position that needs to be filled, and I inspire and empower them to succeed beyond their greatest expectations (#2). I foster positive attitudes toward our company, and model healthy workplace relationships (#3). I give this by encouraging, supporting (#4), and motivating people to exceed what they thought was possible (#5).

Rachel and Josh listened attentively as they followed along with Ron. Then, there was an uncomfortable silence, which the formerly quiet and reticent Josh finally interrupted.

"Ron, you said that you're CEO of World Wide Synergistics. But you're currently VP of Sales, and we're both hoping to serve the company under you. So what is the CEO stuff about?"

Rachel nodded. "Yeah, I want to know, too. I don't get it."

"Fair enough," Ron replied. "The reality is, I rewrite my statement fresh every year. Sometimes even more often. The previous one I wrote said, 'I am the VP of Sales at World Wide Synergistics.' So, when I reached that position, I drafted a new statement. You see, your personal Authentic Brand Statement is really your personal view of who you are and where you want to be. Essentially, it is who you are and who you are becoming, but it is still solidly based on the greatest leadership gift that you have to give right here and now. It's basically an honest 'no baloney' assessment of your past, your present, and the future you desire. So, in the first sentence, I said, 'I am the CEO,' because I believe that is essential to who I am . . . and destined to become. It is the core of my Authenticity Code™. Remember, the code is Your Presence + Your Audience + Your Presentation = Your Success. Your Authentic Brand Statement is the core of *Your Presence*—what makes you truly you. It identifies what you want to be known for, how you want to be seen, and who you are as a leader or professional."

Rachel couldn't wait to make an observation. "Are you saying that we need to write our own Authentic Brand Statements? And even be free to express our dreams, our vision, of the future? That this is somehow significant to getting a promotion and solidifying our careers?"

"In a way, it is. It's that important, so, yes, as part of this process, I will be asking both of you to write your statements. I'm sure you realize that there is no point in beginning a journey without having *some* destination as a goal. The destination may ultimately change over time, but the initial destination is a vital place to begin."

Rachel nodded and said, "I think I know exactly what you're saying. On a recent business trip to New York, I thought it would be fun to board a subway train and go somewhere. I had no destination in mind. Luckily, I was on a southbound train and ended up in Greenwich Village. I discovered some fun spots and met some wonderful people! But, at the time, I was clueless. The next time I visit Manhattan, I will plan to go to the Village to look up my new friends. And if I don't find them, I'll make even newer friends."

"That's a good story," Ron replied. "And it indicates that you can adapt to whatever situation you face. I think that's a great trait to have."

"Why is that a great trait?" Josh wondered aloud.

"It's important, I think, because adaptation is a crucial element of authenticity. If you are stuck in a job or career you hate, you either have to change your attitude, change your situation, or change your career. Many people are not truly authentic until they embrace change."

Rachel chimed in again. "So, what you're telling us is that adaptation may be a key part of authenticity?"

"Of course," Ron agreed. "It's also a key part of an effective presentation. The purpose behind many—if not most—presentations is to influence key decision makers to make a decision, to take action, or to buy into your proposal. To accomplish that objective, you have to know your audience. You may even have to adapt to your audience. In Disney terms, that means you might have to select hair color that looks natural. You may not be able to choose bright purple hair when you are playing Moana. You have to consider your chosen audience because you authentically chose to serve that audience."

"Is that all it takes?" Josh asked.

"Of course not. There is quite often a time factor imposed on you. You may be asked to give a 20-minute presentation, but it may be cut to 5 minutes just before you're scheduled to start. Maybe the meeting is running long."

"Wow, that could present a difficult situation," Rachel said.

"Yeah, that would really throw me off," Josh added.

"Not to worry," Ron continued. "In one of our upcoming sessions, I'll give you the very clear secret on how to handle that *if* and *when* it happens."

Rachel and Josh nodded. "Great!" they said together.

"But I still have a question about the Authentic Brand Statement," Josh said.

"Shoot!" Ron grinned.

"Do you have some kind of definition of what it really is?"

"Yes, of course. Your Authentic Brand Statement is really *your most powerful way of adding value by expressing your unique gifts and talents.* It is a statement that describes what you came here to do and who you came here to be.

"First, it's vital that you dig for the answers to the questions I have listed on the sixth and seventh pages of your handout packet.

"Your Authentic Brand Statement will reveal answers to the three essential questions at the top of the page. You answer ten very specific questions that when combined will uncover your brand statement and success factors for living your brand.

"The first five questions are part one of your brand statement, and the second five questions are part two."

"AUTHENTIC BRAND STATEMENT" KEY QUESTIONS:

1. What do you want to be known for?

2. How do you want to be seen?

3. Who are you as a leader?

AUTHENTIC BRAND STATEMENT: PART I

Your most powerful way of adding value by expressing your unique gifts and talents.

Q

1. What is the ONE professional/leadership role I most want to hold?
(e.g., Executive, philanthropist, CFO, vice president, author, technical fellow, role model leader, program manager, coach, parent, CEO, Sales representative, board member, business owner, catalyst, etc.)

A

Q

2. What is the ONE THING I most want to do/accomplish as I work in my desired role?
(e.g., Successfully lead a new program, empower employees to turn around a failing program/product, invent a new product/service, help change a corporate culture, etc.)

A

Q

3. What is the ONE THING I most want to change as I work in my desired role?
(e.g., Financial loss—turn a company around; my presence—become calm and peaceful; negative relationships—foster healthy workplace relationships; etc.)

A

Q

4. What is the ONE THING I most wish my parents would have given me growing up?
(e.g., Seen and celebrated my unique gifts and talents, modeled a healthy relationship, listened to my point of view, unconditionally accepted me, etc.)

A

Q

5. What is the ONE THING I know I have as a professional/leadership strength that comes naturally to me?
(e.g., Providing a safe environment for everyone to speak their truth, inspiring people to give their 100 percent, setting a clear vision that many follow, etc.)

A

Ron had them take a break from the handouts. "You may have noticed that I answered the first five questions in my Authentic Brand Statement."

Rachel responded, "Yes, that was really clear."

"How about your personal answers to questions six through ten?" Josh asked. "What is the difference between part one and part two?"

Ron replied, "Part one is your brand statement, and part two is how you measure whether you are successfully living your brand statement. In other words, part two is your authentic brand success criteria. Take a look at the questions for part two."

AUTHENTIC BRAND STATEMENT: PART 2
Success criteria for living your authentic brand statement.

6. What is the one thing I most want to SEE as I work in my desired role?
(e.g. My protégés all getting promoted, my organization transforming into my vision, me making a big program sale for my company/organization, me achieving all my goals and objectives, etc.)

7. What is the one thing I most want to HEAR as I work in my desired role?
(e.g., "You helped me transform my life," "Without you we would have failed," "You are the best boss," "You helped increase profits by 50 percent," "You are the best team player." etc.)

8. What is the one thing I most want to EXPERIENCE as I work in my desired role?
(e.g., Going to bed and waking up on a daily basis knowing I am making a difference; leading a high-performing team; being recognized as a leading expert in my field; complete fulfillment in my work; etc.)

9. What is the one thing I most want to SAY as I work in my desired role?
(e.g., "I have made the difference I wanted to make and have no regrets," "Listen, I have something important to say," "I am the happiest I have ever been," "We need to pull together and get this done," "I balanced a great career and personal life," etc.)

10. What is the one thing I want to FEEL as I work in my desired role?
(e.g., Proud of the life I have lived and the legacy I have left, happy and fulfilled in my life, confident that I gave my all, satisfied with the business results I achieved, etc.)

Josh was quick to ask, "Can you give us your answers to those questions?"

"I'd be happy to do that," Ron replied. "In fact, if you turn to the next page, you'll find them in black and white. I refer to it as 'But Wait . . . There's More.'"

BUT WAIT . . . THERE'S MORE!

- The one thing I want to SEE as the CEO is that this company performs in alignment with my highest vision for it.

- What I most want to HEAR as the CEO is "You helped me transform my career and my life!"

- The thing I most want to EXPERIENCE as the CEO is the positive feeling that comes from "a job well done!" (Not just well done by me, but by the entire team.)

- The thing I most want to SAY as the CEO is "Thanks to all of you team members and your dedication, we are indisputably the leaders in our industry."

- The single most important thing I want to FEEL is pride in the life I have lived and the legacy I have left.

Rachel smiled at this exciting revelation.

"See, hear, experience, say, feel," she said. "Those all *do* sound to me like specific ways that you measure how successful you are at living out your authentic brand."

"You are so right," Ron answered. "While it is important to have clear goals, it is equally important to have clear ways of knowing you have met your goals. Of course, this is a continuous, ongoing process. When you achieve one of your success criteria, you can write a new one. When you achieve your brand statement, you can redo the entire ten-question exercise."

Rachel glanced at her watch. This first meeting had run over, and she had things to do. "So, what's the next step?" she asked.

"Your next step is to use the new information you have learned to craft your Authentic Brand Statement. Refer to the next two pages as your guide.

"After you fill in your answers to these ten questions, your task is to draft your Authentic Brand Statement using your answers.

"As you can see, there is a straightforward form you can use."

PART 1:
MY AUTHENTIC BRAND STATEMENT:

(Insert Your Answers from the Previous Part 1 Statements in the Following Spaces.)

I am a _____ (insert #1)

who _____

_____ (insert #2)

I _____

_____ (insert #3)

I give this by _____

_____

_____ (insert #4 and #5)

HERE IS ANOTHER "PART 1:
AUTHENTIC BRAND STATEMENT" EXAMPLE:

I am a role model leader (#1) who teaches others how to be better leaders through leading by example (#2). I interact without judging or becoming defensive (#3). I give this by understanding individual choices, making wise decisions, and meeting my commitments (#4 and #5).

PART 2:
SUCCESS CRITERIA FOR LIVING MY BRAND STATEMENT:

(Insert Your Answers from the Previous Part 2 Statements in the Following Spaces.)

1. See _____ (insert #6)

2. Hear _____ (insert #7)

3. Experience _____ (insert #8)

4. Say _____ (insert #9)

5. Feel _____ (insert #10)

EXAMPLE PART 2: SUCCESS CRITERIA
(FOLLOWING ARE POINTS 6 TO 10 IN THE PREVIOUS EXAMPLE)

1. **See** people become great leaders because they modeled me. #6

2. **Hear** people say that I was the best leader they ever had. #7

3. **Experience** a great big party with a room full of people who thought I made a difference in their lives. #8

4. **Say** "Wow, I balanced a great career and personal life with no regrets of either." #9

5. **Feel** that I would not have changed a thing about my career and personal life balance. #10

"If you carefully study all of these points, you will likely notice that they are focused more on your presence and less on presentation," Ron observed. "This is an important distinction, because without the component of authentic presence, your actual formal or informal presentation or communication will often fall flat."

Josh looked to be fully invested in both the examples and the discussion, something that Ron again noticed. And it put a smile on Ron's face!

"Will we be giving our Authentic Brand Statements to you at our next meeting?" Rachel and Josh both wondered aloud.

"No, our meetings over the next few weeks will cover the next four key points of making effective, compelling presentations. Of course, I'll be mixing in some of the key points of authentic presence so that the big picture emerges. I will also be asking another key teammate to join us for some of those meetings."

Josh and Rachel stood and headed toward the door, thinking the meeting was over.

But Ron called after them, "One more thing. I want you to begin working on your own Authentic Brand Statements. You'll be sharing them as part of your last formal presentation to me."

TAKE A MOMENT . . .

Now is the perfect time for you to begin working on your Authentic Brand Statement. Start by filling in your answers to part one, questions one through five, on page 41, then part two, questions six through ten, on page 42. If you prefer, you can download a clean copy of this exercise at insideoutlearning.com/yourauthenticbrand.

Then simply take your answers to the ten questions and use them to fill in the following form.

For question three identify what you most want to change and then put it in the form of a positive. For example, if you most want to change negative workplace relationships, then write down "Foster Healthy Workplace Relationships" as your answer to number three.

If you have trouble answering question four, remember that your parents did the best they could with the knowledge and experience they had at the time. This question is nothing against your parents. It is a profound insight that what we most wanted to receive from our parents or authority figures while we were growing up is what we most have to give. In other words, our greatest wound is actually our greatest gift to give to the world.

For example, I always wanted my parents to see my unique gifts and talents. What I most wanted to receive is what I most have to give. Even in developing these ten questions, I am expressing my greatest gift by helping you get in touch with your unique gifts and talents.

If question four does not work for you, don't worry and just go with what you write down in question five.

MY FIRST ATTEMPT AT PART I:
MY AUTHENTIC BRAND STATEMENT:

I am a _____ (insert #1)

who _____

_____ (insert #2)

I _____

_____

_____ (insert #3)

I give this by _____

_____

_____ (insert #4 and #5)

PART 2:
SUCCESS CRITERIA FOR LIVING MY BRAND STATEMENT:

1. See _____ (insert #6)

2. Hear _____ (insert #7)

3. Experience _____ (insert #8)

4. Say _____ (insert #9)

5. Feel _____ (insert #10)

7

There Is More to Authenticity
Than the Presentation

A WEEK LATER, RACHEL and Josh had just taken their places in Ron's office and settled in for their next abbreviated APPS-based training session when the "special guest" Ron had indicated would join them walked into the room.

He introduced her. "I'm sure you both know our VP of Human Resources, Victoria Reynolds."

Josh and Rachel nodded affirmatively.

Ron continued, "What you may not know about Ms. Reynolds is that she is actually Dr. Reynolds, and she is a former college professor who taught in the fields of psychology and human development. Dr. Reynolds, would you like to say a few words?"

"Thanks, Ron. I am here today only because Ron asked me for my input on the important decision he faces. Although the decision as to who is selected for the associate director of Sales is entirely up to him, he has told me about you both and what a difficult choice this will be for him. Because I am the one who originally introduced The Authenticity Code™ and the APPS program to our company, he felt it could be helpful if I would join you for this training session and then provide my coaching experience to you before you make your next presentations."

"I think that's a great idea," Rachel noted. "I need all the help I can get."

"Me too," Josh quickly added.

Ron and Victoria nodded, pleased by both candidates' openness to coaching.

"Here's a little quiz," Ron said as he began the session. "Can either of you tell me what the main point of our first meeting was?"

Rachel jumped on it. "I think the main point was that it's important to draft our own Authentic Brand Statement to help us to plan and guide our future. And we use IOL's Style Recognition Assessment to help us determine who we really are."

Ron chuckled. "Okay, our first meeting tended to wander through the wilderness a bit, so I can easily see why you came to that conclusion. We have covered some things about your audience and presence so far, and now we need to get into the presentation."

Josh, growing ever bolder, suddenly spoke. "Ron . . . Dr. Reynolds . . .

"Please call me 'Victoria.'"

"Okay, Victoria." Josh began again. "Ron, Victoria, I have a stupid question."

Everyone laughed a bit, but Ron immediately replied: "Josh, there is no such thing as a 'stupid question.' I believe that there are only worthy, honest questions that deserve to be answered honestly."

"Okay," Josh continued. "Here's my 'worthy, honest question.' When it comes to what you call The Authenticity Code™, which component is the most important? Is it *presence* or *audience* or *presentation*? Which one ultimately leads to *success*?"

"Nothing stupid about that question," Ron said, an ear-to-ear grin on his face. "In fact, I've been patiently waiting for one of you to ask it."

"Good job, Josh!" Rachel whispered in affirmation.

Josh beamed and whispered back, "Thanks."

Victoria suggested, "Why don't you answer that great question, Ron?"

Ron responded, "The most direct answer is that all three are of equal importance. Miss one component, and authenticity doesn't have a chance. It is difficult to separate the three parts of The Authenticity Code™ because your presence + your audience + your presentation all are critically important for success, and they mix together."

"I don't understand," Josh admitted. "How can that be?"

Ron thought for a moment. "Okay, the best example of how this works is a smoothie."

"A smoothie?" Rachel and Josh asked at the same time.

"You've lost me," the usually astute Victoria confessed.

Ron laughed. "Okay, I admit this may be a bit random for you, but I begin every day with a healthy, energy-boosting smoothie. I make it in a Vitamix blender, although there are several other good brands on the market."

"More information, please," Josh coaxed.

"You got it! My smoothies are made of whatever healthy stuff I have in my fridge: bananas, blueberries, strawberries, kiwi, celery, and leafy greens, such as kale."

"Kale?" Josh replied incredulously. "YUCK! That stuff reminds me of sandpaper!"

"Yeah, I think so, too. But when it's thoroughly blended with the other ingredients, it's not only delicious; it's also energizing! It offers significant health benefits. When I combine them in the blender, I achieve my desired outcome. I get the nutrients my body needs.

"It's much the same when it comes to the 'ingredients' of The Authenticity Code™. They have to be combined—blended together—to achieve maximum effectiveness. It truly is the art and science of success. I'll be teaching you how to follow the formula for presentation success, practice the authentic presence qualities, and tailor your message to your audience. All of this part of The Authenticity Code™ is the science of success because there are formulas and guidelines to follow. The part of The Authenticity Code™ that is the art of success is when you finally realize that *you* are the presentation and when you exhibit your authentic brand in all that you do. You truly cannot fake it to make it because anyone can spot a phony!"

"That's exactly right," Victoria agreed. "I think about great communicators like the Reverend Dr. Martin Luther King Jr. I have studied his remarkable—but far too short—life. He was truly authentic!

"Dr. King was the leader who taught us—in the horrible, challenging context of pre–Civil Rights Act America—the hope that people, including his four little children, would one day live in a nation where they would 'not be judged by the color of their skin but by the content of their character.'"

Rachel was excited. "I love that landmark speech! I admire Dr. King so much, and I have repeatedly watched his 'I Have a Dream' speech. It was magnificent!"

Ron picked it up from there. "It really was! What made Dr. King authentic is that his words, his beliefs, and his actions all matched perfectly. His mission was positive, nonviolent change. That's what he said, that's what he believed, and that is how he lived his life.

"He also had a stunning presence. He *looked* like a leader. He 'dressed the part.' He had style, class, and manners. That's who he was!

"On top of that, he knew his audience. He knew that so many in this nation had felt beaten down in the aftermath of the Civil War. They believed they had not truly been freed—that their basic human rights were being unfairly denied. He knew that his task was to inspire people to believe and hope . . . to motivate them and unite them. He knew that anything less would lead to their despair.

"Finally, he knew the power of a clear presentation. He spoke with confidence, clarity, and authority. He repeated his underlying theme so effectively that it could not be ignored."

Victoria had a related thought. "To me, many of the other thoughts and ideas Dr. King communicated were as significant as his 'I Have a Dream' speech. My favorite quote of his is 'A man dies when he refuses to take a stand for that which is true.'"

"That is a wonderful quote, and, of course, that's a great illustration," Rachel effused.

"Dr. King is such a great example of demonstrating authentic presence and presentation skills. It would also be helpful to have a corporate example," Josh added.

Ron paused briefly as he thought further. "Okay, here's one that is a more recent business example. I was at a conference in Australia, and an American corporate speaker ran down the auditorium aisles with loud music playing, and he started dancing on stage at the beginning of his presentation. He then asked everyone in the audience to clap and dance with him. This was an immediate turnoff to the audience. He had not done his homework on the Australian culture. Many Australians do not like or appreciate flashy, loud, 'standout' presenters. They like to get to the point quickly and really do not like showy people or presentations.

"I immediately noticed that no one was listening to what this presenter had to say. In fact, many left the room, and I saw a lot of eye-rolling during his presentation, which incorporated lots of loud audio files and sounds. He got the lowest approval rating of any speaker at the conference.

"In the United States, his presentation was received really well, and it was clear and concise. But he lost his international audience. This demonstrates that you can have a good presentation, but if you don't tailor your message to your audience—and match your presence to your audience—then you disconnect from your audience. His flashiness and showiness were a complete distraction to his Australian audience, so much so that his intended message was not heard. He did not take the time in advance to know his audience, which is the first step in making a successful presentation.

"This demonstrates that you can have a solid, clear presentation, but if your presence and delivery do not align with your audience, you lose them."

"That doesn't seem authentic to me," Rachel interjected. "It feels as though you're teaching us to be someone we're not, just to please the audience."

"I understand how you would think that. In reality, it's your authentic choice what audience you choose to present to. That speaker chose to go to Australia and be in front of that business-minded audience. That was an authentic choice. Your purpose as a communicator is to move, motivate, inspire, and, most of all, *serve* your audience. You *can* show up authentic in who you are with a clear, inspiring presentation *for* your audience. This speaker showed up for himself, not his audience. He did not do his homework prior to the presentation and answer the four questions in the audience-understanding matrix that we talked about in our first meeting."

Josh said, "Now I get it. What you're saying is that if the presenter did not want to modify his flashy style for his keynote presentation to the Australian audience, he could have chosen not to present to that audience."

"Yes, you did get it, Josh!"

"Thank you, Ron," Rachel chimed in. "That's new thinking for me, to see it as an authentic choice to deliberately decide what audiences we present to and interact with.

"I have a question, though. Wouldn't it help us in our presentations to you if we knew what your answers were to the four audience-understanding questions you asked us previously in our first session?"

"Yes, that would absolutely help," Ron agreed. "However, I'd really like to hear your thoughts."

"Okay. Josh, what do you think is most important to Ron?" Rachel asked.

"Hmm. I think it's important that Ron is confident that he can make a sound decision when it comes to choosing one of us. So, I think we'll both have to give him the information and assurance he needs."

"That's really good," Rachel replied. "If you remember his Authentic Brand Statement, he said something about seeking out and hiring the most competent, skilled, innovative individuals for every position that needs to be filled. He said, 'I inspire and empower them to succeed beyond their greatest expectations. I foster positive attitudes toward our company and model healthy workplace relationships. I give this by encouraging, supporting, and motivating people to exceed what they thought was possible.'"

"That sounds perfect," Josh said.

"I'm a good notetaker," Rachel responded. "I picked up that skill in college."

"You really are, Rachel. And it's a good skill to have," Ron said.

Josh continued: "Answering these questions before we start to prepare a presentation is a critical step. The answers help us learn how the key decision makers make their decisions, as well as what information they need to respond positively to our message or say yes to the point of the presentation."

Rachel said, "Good point. We still need to answer the three other questions for Ron. The second question according to my notes is 'What details does he need?'"

Josh answered: "He told us that in the feedback he gave us after our first failed attempt at presenting to him. He thought you presented too many details and I did not present enough detail. Therefore, I believe he needs enough detail to fill the time period and meet the objective of the presentation, but not too much detail that you go over the time allotted."

"Exactly correct!" Ron confirmed again.

Rachel continued with the third question. "What do you think hooks Ron? I know that, because it is in his Authentic Brand Statement. He loves to hire competent, innovative, skilled individuals and inspire and empower them. So, I think that if we show we are competent, innovative, skilled, and empowered, it would hook him."

Josh replied, "Right on, Rachel." Ron beamed, proud for how well his protégés were doing with answering the audience-understanding matrix questions.

Josh said, "I remember the fourth and final question—what is Ron willing to compromise? And I know the answer to that. He would put quality before schedule or cost because he is willing to take the extra time and expense to help us both be successful."

"Wow, I am so impressed by how well you analyzed me as your key decision maker," Ron said. "It shows me you're really listening and taking this to heart."

"But I have a question," Rachel interjected. "How do we know the answers to these questions if the key decision makers haven't told us or we don't know them personally?"

"Great question," Ron said. "You can ask people who know the decision maker. You could ask those in the inner circle. For example, you know that Victoria is in my inner circle because I invited her here today, so you might want to ask her more about what she notices about me as an audience member. You could also ask any one of my direct reports because many of them have worked with me for years—first as peers and now as a part of my vital inner circle."

Rachel said, "That would work for me."

"Me too," Josh replied. "But what about also playing CLUE and guessing their preferred personality style and then tailoring the message to their style?"

"Fair question," Ron admitted. "I already gave you a handout on IOL's style recognition clues for each of the four personality styles: point people, people people, planner people, and party people. So I would always be looking for these clues in every interaction you have with your decision maker. Before your presentation, you can also show the decision maker or one of his or her key followers the descriptions of each style and ask if they would feel comfortable sharing the decision maker's preferred style.

"If you don't know, then you must ensure that your presentation includes language that appeals to all four styles. If you only present in your personally established preference, you could lose your audience if they don't share that communication preference. What I am now handing you is gold. I keep IOL's clue sheet and this sheet labeled 'Adapting to Others' Styles' on my cell phone and next to my computer. I am constantly looking for clues with everyone I interact with. Once you do a best guess of their preferred style, then you refer to this sheet on how to adapt your language to that style."

STYLE RECOGNITION: ADAPTING TO OTHERS' STYLES

Think about your key audience members or someone you have trouble communicating with.

Determine which style best represents that person.

Plan your next interaction with that audience/person and use the tips.

Use the tool again to plan a conversation with another audience/person.

To adapt to People People

Be warm and sincere by

- Supporting their feelings by showing personal interest when possible
- Assuming they'll take things personally
- Allowing them time to trust you
- Discussing personal feelings—not facts—when you disagree
- Moving along in a slower, informal, but casual steady manner
- Showing that you're actively listening

To adapt to Party People

Show interest in them by

- Supporting their opinions, ideas, and dreams when possible
- Being upbeat, stimulating, and fast-paced
- Tolerating digressions and not hurrying a discussion
- Trying not to argue—you'll seldom win
- Being enthusiastic, spontaneous, and casual
- Explaining how action can enhance their image
- Sparing them the details

To adapt to Planner People

Show yourself to be thorough by

- Supporting their organized, thoughtful approach when possible
- Showing commitment through your actions, not just words
- Being detailed, accurate, and logical
- Listing advantages and disadvantages of any plan organized
- Providing solid, tangible evidence
- Adhering to established procedures
- Giving assurances that decisions won't backfire on them

To adapt to Point People

Be efficient and competent by

- Supporting their goals and objectives when possible
- Keeping your relationship businesslike
- Using facts—not personal feelings—if you disagree
- Being precise, effective, and well organized
- Recommending alternative actions with brief supporting analyses
- Getting to the point quickly
- Stressing competitive results and growth opportunities

Josh and Rachel both studied the chart carefully.

Ron continued, "If your detective work in searching for clues leads you to believe that you are presenting to a people person, you speak their language by supporting their feelings; showing personal interest; allowing them time to trust you; discussing personal feelings; moving along in a slower, informal, but casual steady manner; and showing that you're actively listening. Remember, if you don't know your audience's type or you know your audience is mixed types, then you need to make sure your presentation hits all four types of language.

"Rachel, you presented to me in your initial presentation as if I were a people person, but my main preference is a point person, so you lost me. Do you see now why that was the case?"

Rachel said, "Yes, I do, Ron, because you wanted me to get to the point quickly; present facts; be precise, effective, and well organized; keep the presentation businesslike; support your goals and objectives; recommend alternative actions with a brief supporting analysis; and stress competitive results and growth opportunities."

Ron smiled. "You got it, Rachel. I can't tell you how many times people lose their audience by presenting according to their own preferred style instead of the key decision maker's preferred style. This is what tailoring your message to your audience is all about. Yet I don't want you to stop being a people person. Share with me your volunteer experience, and maybe share one story instead of ten."

After Rachel and Josh took a minute to absorb the handout, Ron continued, "That's why the style recognition tool is so important. It helps us learn how the key decision makers make their decisions, as well as what information they need to respond positively to our message or say yes to the point of the presentation. The style recognition, together with the four questions on the audience-understanding matrix, makes up the *your audience* part of The Authenticity Code™. When you take The Authenticity Code™—APPS—program, you'll also learn about key tools and techniques for reading your audience during a presentation, and effectively fielding audience questions. You will also take an additional personality assessment, which is a more advanced tool that also helps you tailor your message to your audience."

Rachel and Josh both said they'd take the program the next time it was offered.

Ron continued, "I recently learned that 70 percent of the US population are Sensors on the Myers-Briggs and need an agenda to follow a presentation, so I always recommend having one. The other 30 percent, who are Intuitive on the Myers-Briggs, will ignore it, but you will lose the 70 percent majority without an agenda. I find this type of information fascinating."

"After working on your presence and tailoring your message to your audience, the next solution revolves around honing your presentation skills to be as engaging, compelling, and persuasive as possible. And that's what we will be discussing today. And remember, the *your presentation* part of The Authenticity Code™ can mean a formal or informal presentation or any communication you prepare for and want to influence a key decision maker—even a job interview is a presentation of you and your skills."

The expressions on the candidates' faces told Ron that Josh and Rachel were eager to dig in, so he continued, "Do you recall in our first meeting that most key decision makers prefer to receive their information in BLUF format?"

"Yes," Josh replied. "'Bottom line up front.' In movie terms, that would mean 'cut to the chase.'"

"Well, yes and no," Ron answered. "It's still important to set up the chase scene to make it clear why the chase is important to the movie in the first place."

"Great point, Ron!" Victoria agreed without hesitation.

Ron continued, "So, today, our plan is to cram a lot of significant information into a short period of time. We'll start with the first step to presentation success, after 'Know Your Audience,' of course. Please always remember you start with knowing your audience and then writing a presentation in a way that will inspire your audience."

Ron distributed a new handout that presented this list:

THE FORMULA FOR PRESENTATION SUCCESS . . .
ONCE YOU KNOW YOUR AUDIENCE

- Deliver an Attention-Getting Opening
- Focus on a Clear Executive Summary
- Develop an Agenda with a Concise Body Message
- Finish Strong

Rachel and Josh gave the form a quick once-over as Ron pointed out the obvious: "I'm sure that you've noticed that I've allowed considerable blank space between the key points."

"For taking notes," Josh suggested.

"Exactly! In fact, you may need to continue your notes on the back side of the sheet, in your notebooks, or on your laptops or cell phones. As I said, we have a lot to cover over the next few weeks so you can crack The Authenticity Code™ and understand the art and science of success."

8

The Next Key to a Compelling Presentation

"**O**NCE YOU HAVE completed your audience-understanding matrix and know some basics about your audience," Ron said, "you need to plan and rehearse an attention-getting opening that will hook them to listen to you. So again, this meeting is all about the *your presentation* part of The Authenticity Code™.

"When an army drill sergeant stands in front of a group of new recruits and yells something like 'Ten-hut, maggots,' you'd better believe that those recruits are immediately paying attention to that 'opening.' Any other response could lead to 100 push-ups, or any of a number of other unpleasant outcomes.

"But, as a leader, presenter, teacher, or speaker, you have to employ different tactics. You must command a different level of attention. You need to project another kind of presence.

"The reality is, when you begin a speech, a sales pitch, a job interview, or any other type of presentation, you only have 90 to 120 seconds to 'grab' your audience. There are a number of time-tested ways to accomplish this daunting feat."

Josh fired up his sleek laptop and said, "Ready."

Rachel took out her notebook and pen. "Ready here."

Ron ran down his memorized list. "The first way to grab attention is through a *story*. Personal stories are usually the most effective. Stories about your own experience or someone else's experience—or even stories about the success or failure of a project that relates to your topic—are all very powerful.

"The second way to command attention is through *humor*. That being said, never begin with a joke, even if you think it won't offend anyone in your audience. Even self-deprecating humor often backfires. For example, if you talk about being overweight yourself, anyone else in your audience who thinks he or she is overweight may not find that funny or engaging.

"Instead, consider using a Dilbert cartoon . . . an *image* or series of images. One well-known speaker I know—Mark Victor Hansen, cocreator of the best-selling *Chicken Soup for the Soul* book series—likes to flash some audience-appropriate cartoons on the screen at the beginning of his presentations. It's his version of humor. In general, captivating images that relate to your subject matter are best. Appropriate visual images can get the attention of your audience quickly. Of course, don't ever use copyrighted material without written permission. And, depending on how you intend to use the material, you may have to pay a fee to the copyright owner.

"The third way is to use an *analogy* or *metaphor*." Ron looked at his own computer screen. "Here is the definition of *analogy* from Vocabulary.com: 'When you draw an analogy between two things, you compare them for the purpose of explanation. The movie character Forrest Gump made a silly analogy famous: "Life is like a box of chocolates."' I believe that the more unusual or humorous the analogy, the more effective it will be.

"A solid fourth way to capture your audience's attention is by asking a *question*. If you think you have a friendly, spirited audience, you could ask a relevant question of the group as a whole. You can also ask three questions, with the first two being 'no' questions where few people will raise their hands, and then a 'yes' question that will get everyone to raise their hands. However, I do not recommend calling on people with raised hands—because you will be giving control to the audience right from the start. Of course, you could always *plant an audience member there* with a question that you know will support your presentation. Also, be sure to give your audience some time to answer your question, at least in their minds.

"The fifth and final attention-getting technique on my short list is to begin with a *quotation*. People enjoy hearing the thoughts of other people expressed in memorable ways. Everyone remembers when John F. Kennedy said, 'Ask not what your country can do for you—ask what you can do for your country.' Your quote doesn't need to be serious, as long as it's relevant. So, it can be a quote from a movie or a cartoon or a book. Think of the *Apollo 13* film based on a real event: 'Houston, we have a problem.'"

"Those all make sense to me," Rachel observed.

"As you might guess, there are other components to your opening. This is where you 'tell your audience what you are going to tell them.' Turn to the next page, and you'll see what you need to keep in mind to take advantage of the attention you've captured."

KEY THOUGHTS TO CONSIDER:

- Don't be vague. Get straight to your point! (Don't leave it to your audience to figure it out. Do it for them. That's *your* job!)

- All effective communicators start crisply . . .

- You only have one chance at a first impression. Richard Branson makes up his mind about people in 30 seconds. In your first 90–120 seconds, your audience is making a multitude of decisions about you and your presentation.

The beginning has to rivet the interest of the audience. More than any other part of the presentation, every detail should be carefully planned. This is the time for you to set their expectations and establish your credibility. Your first words would ideally be like a tasty appetizer that whets their appetite and interests them in the full-course meal. Make it short, fast, punchy, interesting, and creative.

Ron concluded the session with some additional thoughts: "Think about a presentation you have attended sometime in the past.

"Did the presenter make an immediate positive impression on you?

"Why?

"What did the presenter do or say to 'hook' you from the beginning?

"Was the main point clear to you?

"These are the things I want you to consider seriously as you prepare for 'round two' of your presentations to me and Victoria."

With that admonition, Ron stood up, faced everyone, and did a snappy military salute.

"Dis-missed! See you next week. Same time, same place."

"Got it, sir!" they all responded as they left the room.

TAKE A MOMENT . . .

Think about your next likely (or possible) presentation or interview:

1. Which attention-getting opening might be the most effective and why?

_____

_____

_____

_____

2. Which openings have you used in the past, and how effective were they?

_____

_____

_____

_____

3. What personal stories can you tell that just might relate to audiences in your field?

_____

_____

_____

_____

9

Focus on a Clear
Executive Summary

BEING THE OVERACHIEVER Rachel was, she studied what Ron taught in between the weekly sessions. She started to apply the audience-understanding matrix and attention-getting opening to the presentation she knew she would deliver to try to get the associate director of Sales position—currently the job of her dreams. She understood that Ron was a point person, and started to write her presentation in a crisp, clear, and concise way. She was so grateful to Ron for his time and mentorship and put everything she had into practicing what she was learning. Somehow she managed to do this with her busy work schedule and her volunteer work at the Leukemia and Lymphoma Society.

Meanwhile, Josh truly appreciated his downtime and did not really look at his notes in between the sessions. He did, however, reflect on what he was learning when designing new tech inventions, rebuilding old cars, and reading space and science journals and sci-fi books. This was a great opportunity to grow, and he appreciated Ron for his time, though he realized he had intense competition with Rachel and couldn't help feeling a bit insecure about it: He believed he was not as outgoing or likeable as she was.

The week flew by, and before they knew it, it was time for their next session. Ron wasted no time as he began the weekly meeting. "So, this meeting is about the next step in the formula for presentation success: the 'Executive Summary.'

"You have already announced to your audience *why* you are there to present to them. Now it's time to focus on a clear Executive Summary.

"Very honestly, I've never met any decision maker who doesn't like bullet points. Decision makers are usually busy people who don't have time to waste. In basic Hollywood terms, they want to cut to the chase, as Josh has already suggested.

"That means they want *three specific things*, as you will see in the packet of handouts.

THE THREE COMPONENTS OF AN EFFECTIVE EXECUTIVE SUMMARY:

1. What is the key purpose of your presentation?

2. What's in it for your audience? (This is all about a bottom-line statement that gives the audience reasons to listen—it has nothing to do with you.)

3. When you have finished your "pitch," what do you want the audience to do? (What do you expect? What actions do you want them to take?)

"As you begin, you again have to ask yourself the key question, 'What are the underlying goals of my presentation or communication?'

"The Executive Summary is especially important if your presentation is cut short for some reason. You will discover that, on occasion, you will be told that you have, for example, 20 minutes for your full presentation. But another presenter could run long, and you could be informed at the last instant that you will only have five minutes. That's when a clear, concise Executive Summary comes into play. There are three key parts of an effective Executive Summary:

"First, you state your *purpose*. In many cases, it is to *educate* or *inform*. You might be giving a project or program update, sharing information on a new project or program proposal, describing the value of a product or service, or even sharing why you are the best candidate for a position you are interviewing for.

"Second, state your *value proposition*: What's in it for your audience? Why should they listen to you? What is the bottom-line impact of your presentation? It could be cost savings, market share increase, time and efficiency savings, or some other benefit that the audience will receive from listening to you.

"Third, what is the *desired outcome*? You could be seeking a decision, approval to go to the next step, additional resources, input or feedback, help solving a problem, or help in the process of moving forward to the next step."

Rachel jumped in right away. "I want to make sure I understand this part. In order to convince you that I am the right one to be promoted to the position of associate director of Sales, my Executive Summary for you should include the following:

"First, my *purpose* is to inform you what my skills are so you know that I can handle this new position. I believe I am the perfect fit.

"Second, my *value proposition* is that my presentation will help you make the best and most-informed decision. Choosing me will help you perpetuate your positive reputation for developing others and selecting the right people for the right jobs.

"Finally, my *desired outcome* is to gain your confidence to the extent that you will choose me for this promotion, as well as other promotions when you become CEO of World Wide Synergistics!"

Ron grinned from ear to ear when he heard Rachel's closing comment. "I think you've got it, Rachel! How about you, Josh?"

Josh paused for just a moment. "Well . . . I guess if I want this promotion, I'll have to follow Rachel's lead. . . ."

Victoria quickly added her thoughts: "Or, Josh, you could demonstrate your own leadership qualities by developing your personal take on the Executive Summary."

Josh said, "Well, I suppose I could do that."

Ron and Victoria glanced at each other, appearing to question Josh's response. Their furtive glances did not escape Rachel's view. *Hmm*, she thought. *I wonder if Josh really wants this promotion.*

But Victoria came up with a spur-of-the-moment thought. She faced Rachel directly.

"Rachel, do you have any interests outside of your job at World Wide? Hobbies? Pursuits? Community involvement? Politics?"

Rachel thought for a moment. "Politics? No. Zero interest. Hobbies? I guess I would have to say movies, theater, and photography. Community involvement? I got involved with the Leukemia and Lymphoma Society in college. Long story, really, but I'm still involved today. LLS is my charitable cause of choice."

"That's wonderful!" Victoria said.

Rachel continued, "As a matter of fact, I have been invited to present a brief testimonial speech at their annual convention. I consider it to be a real honor."

"Even better," Victoria affirmed. "Would you be willing to do a five-minute summary of your planned presentation at our meeting next week?"

"I sure would," Rachel instantly agreed.

"Great!" Victoria then turned her attention to Josh. She could tell by the look on his face that he was feeling left out. "How about you, Josh? Would you like to reserve five minutes to do your own presentation? Any subject would be okay."

Josh didn't even have to think about his response. "No, thanks. I'll pass." Rachel was clearly an extrovert who loved to present in front of a room. Josh believed he was a strong introvert who had a few close relationships but would rather do almost anything besides presenting in front of a room. He thought he was great at presenting his words clearly in writing but feared oral presentations. He understood why the fear of public speaking was one of the greatest human fears.

Even though Ron was disappointed that Josh said no to an opportunity to present and receive feedback, he knew not to push him in that moment. Ron spoke next to conclude the meeting. "Okay, it's settled. Rachel will do a five-minute presentation at our next meeting. Josh, be prepared to critique her talk."

TAKE A MOMENT...

Think about your next likely (or possible) presentation or interview:

1. What might be your most effective Executive Summary (remember to include the three components—your purpose, your value proposition, and your desired outcome)?

_____

_____

_____

_____

_____

2. If you were asked to tell an audience of 500 professionals about your career (or desired career), what would your Executive Summary be?

_____

_____

_____

_____

3. If you were given the opportunity to give a presentation to the audience of your choice on any topic of your choice, who would be in the audience, and what would your topic be? I encourage you to do it!

_____

_____

_____

_____

10

Rachel's Extra Opportunity

RACHEL COULDN'T HAVE been more excited about the extra opportunity she had been given to present to Ron and Victoria. She used every free minute in her day (and in her evenings at home) to think about and prepare for her presentation on LLS. She determined that—with the five minutes allocated to her—she would have to focus on a brief attention-getting opening, as well as a concise Executive Summary.

The big day arrived, even sooner than she had imagined. *Where did my weekend go?* she wondered.

In the conference room, Ron reminded Victoria and Josh that Rachel was presenting on LLS. With great enthusiasm in his voice, Ron said, "Let's give it up for Rachel!" as he encouraged everyone to applaud.

Rachel stepped up to the podium and began immediately.

"Thank you, Ron!

"This will likely *not* be the most pleasant presentation you will ever hear.

"The brutal truth is, we are all going to die. Hopefully much later than now.

"Some of us will die of heart issues. Some from diabetes. Some possibly from a global pandemic caused by a virus. Some in an automobile accident. So please don't drink and drive!

"But, the truth is, one of the leading causes of death in the United States is cancer. There are many kinds of cancer, of course. But the ones I am here to talk about today are leukemia and lymphoma.

"Both of these awful, dreaded diseases are forms of cancer of the blood.

"Approximately every three minutes one person in the United States is diagnosed with a blood cancer.

"An estimated combined total of 178,520 people in the United States were diagnosed with leukemia, lymphoma, or myeloma in 2020.

"My *purpose* today is to share that new cases of leukemia, lymphoma, and myeloma are expected to account for 10 percent of all new cancer cases diagnosed in the United States.

"Here is my *value proposition*: I believe that, every day, we are getting closer to a cure. These diseases impact too many lives to be relatively obscure. We must push them into the limelight and persist in our goal of finding the cure.

"So, obviously, my *desired outcome* is to move more people to donate funds so more research can be done. I believe that even one death is one too many.

"Thank you for listening to me today!"

Rachel left the podium and returned to her seat.

"Thank you, Rachel," Ron began. "Your presentation was very informative, you adhered to the time limit, and you used the outline for an Executive Summary very effectively. You also used statistics for a very effective attention-getting opening: telling us that every three minutes someone is diagnosed, and giving us the total who were diagnosed in 2020."

"Thank you, Ron," Rachel responded.

Ron turned to Josh. "Have you given any thought to what comments or suggestions you would like to offer?"

"Yes. Rachel, that was really great, well-researched information. And I thought you delivered it with just the right amount of emotion . . . almost enough heartfelt emotion to make me cry. Not quite, but almost. I did get a lump in my throat, though."

"Thank you, Josh," Rachel replied, smiling.

Ron added, "You tugged at my heartstrings, too, Rachel."

Josh wasn't quite finished with his review. "It's really clear to me—and also to Ron and Victoria, I'm sure—that you are fully qualified for this promotion, and you really want it. The truth is, I am the only obstacle standing in your way. And I'm guessing you could leap over me like a two-foot picket fence."

Victoria affirmed that thought. "I agree with your assessment, Josh. Rachel really is qualified for the job. But so are you, and I would like to see you work more on your confidence so you believe in yourself."

Ron added, "I fully agree. The reason I am so adamant about teaching you both The Authenticity Code™ is so that you are fully prepared for any other promotions or job opportunities that may come your way. Authenticity is becoming increasingly important in our competitive world. Employers and managers want to have the confidence that they are hiring and working with the real deal and not someone who is trying to fake it to make it. For that reason, I'd like to continue with our weekly meetings. There are lots of things we have not yet covered."

"We're in," Rachel said.

Josh simply smiled and nodded.

TAKE A MOMENT . . .

1. Volunteering for a charitable organization is a wonderful way to both help your community/the world *and* develop your presentation and presence skills. List the charities/causes that interest you:

_____

_____

_____

_____

2. What do you think that Rachel did *well* in her presentation?

_____

_____

_____

_____

3. What do you think she could have done better to have an even greater effect?

_____

_____

_____

_____

11

Develop an Agenda with a
Concise Body Message

RON BEGAN THE next weekly meeting with an observation. "I'm so glad you're both here today! It appears that you have decided to hang in there with me."

"We have," Rachel agreed, again assuming her new role as "authentic group thought leader."

Josh added, "Of course we're here! It's what any intelligent person who wants to advance in their career would do."

Ron nodded and immediately got to the point of the session. "Assuming that you'll have the opportunity to make your full presentation—and not simply share your Executive Summary—it's time to get even more specific. Your immediate task is always to state your objectives, followed by a clear and concise body message. You're going to tell them what you came there to tell them!

"Your agenda can be likened to a road map—as in 'Here's where we are going'—and your body message includes all of the details, such as 'Travel west on Interstate 10 for 65 miles, until you get to Highway 91. Stay in the right lanes and take Exit 42.'

"By the time you have completed your detailed journey, your audience should have arrived at your intended destination . . . all together and at the same time. *Safely*, I might add!

"Remember, I said 70 percent of the population needs an agenda to follow a presentation, so always have one prepared. An agenda is an outline of your main points. It can be as simple as 'Our Study, Our Findings, and Our Recommendations.' If you happen to be applying for a new job, it could be something such as 'Why Me, Why Here, and Why Now?' Once you have your agenda, here is a simple and memorable aid to develop your clear body message. Follow this straightforward plan, and you will be certain to include all of the key elements you will need. I refer to it as 'HORSE.'"

Josh was already curious. "Horse? I grew up with horses. I love them! I have always enjoyed long trail rides! I still ride any chance I get."

Ron chuckled. "Josh, it's so great to hear you become enthusiastic about this! But this is a different kind of horse. This isn't about trail rides, sorry to say. This horse is more of an acronym. The letters in HORSE represent the first letters of words or phrases intended to remind you to have clarity in each of your agenda items so you can tell your audience what you are there to tell them in a clear and concise way."

"Okay, I'll bite." Josh laughed.

"The *H* in HORSE represents 'Highlight the main point.' In other words, start with the hottest topic. The main point *should* be your best way of capturing the attention of your intended audience. You also always start with your hottest topic in case your presentation is cut short. That way, you at least get your most important topic presented in the time allotted.

"For that reason, when you are pitching to me the reasons why you should be my choice for the promotion, you should plan to start with your strongest point. What do you suppose that point should be?"

Both Rachel and Josh had already begun taking careful notes. But, initially, only Rachel was bold enough to respond.

"In my case," she began, "I'll point out the fact that my enthusiasm for learning and for team play has propelled me toward success in every area of my life."

"What do you mean by that?" Ron asked.

Rachel continued: "In high school, I studied hard and was inducted into the National Honor Society. In college, I joined a sorority and was responsible for our charitable giving budget for four years. In fact, as the leader, I was deeply involved in raising $2.3 million for LLS—the Leukemia and Lymphoma Society. But I've already told you about that in my extra presentation. My participation was motivated by a sorority sister who battled leukemia throughout college. Ultimately, she won the battle!"

"I love a positive outcome!" Josh observed with some actual excitement.

"My plan, then," Rachel continued, "is to offer my presentation in three parts:

"*The Past*: the things I have accomplished previously.

"*The Present*: what I am doing now to help the company.

"*The Future*: what I intend to accomplish in the months and years ahead, should I get the promotion."

"That's wonderful, Rachel! That's a great way to organize and approach it, and when I have finished outlining the entire HORSE concept, you'll see how easily it dovetails with your three main points. Plus, it's clear to me that your enthusiasm could be one of the reasons why you've had such success with social media at World Wide Synergistics. How about you, Josh?"

"Well, yippee for Rachel," Josh said with mock sarcasm.

"That certainly isn't nice, Joshua Armstrong!" Rachel snapped back.

"I know, Rachel. But my story is different from yours. I was a goof-off in high school. No honor society for me. I spent my time on the metal lathe in shop class fabricating cool new parts for the nearly antique 1974 Chevy Corvette my dad gave me. Old, old, old. But General Motors bought my idea for my part and began using it in several of their models when I was a sophomore in high school, because it was still compatible with their latest electronic fuel injection systems. That invention paid my way to Vanderbilt."

"That's a great story, Josh!" Ron interjected.

"Well, yippee for Josh," Rachel added, uncharacteristically.

Ron interrupted: "Hey, you two, stop fighting."

"We're not fighting. We're teasing."

"Exactly," Josh agreed.

"Good. I'll accept that," Ron said. "Let's move on."

"Okay with us," Rachel replied.

"On to the *O*," Ron continued. "The *O* in HORSE stands for 'Okay, so what?'"

Josh couldn't resist. "You're kidding, right?"

Rachel wasn't sure, but she thought she glimpsed a very brief scowl on Ron's face.

"No, Josh, I'm not kidding at all. This is very important."

"I'm sorry. Tell us."

"'Okay, so what' simply means that you tell us exactly *why* your main point—your hottest topic—is important to your listeners. The 'okay' really *is* the 'so what.'

"It is at this point where you will likely state the specific benefits of your plan or proposal.

"Will it save money by reducing costs or increasing efficiency?

"Will it improve the use of time?

"Will it result in a better, more marketable product or service?"

Rachel and Josh each nodded.

"At this point, you are going to emphasize the key meaning of your point—why does it matter? Of course, you can explain verbally, or you can use slides or charts and accomplish the same thing visually.

"Josh, when you invented the doohickey you sold to GM, there must have been a 'so what' that they bought into."

"There sure was!" Josh quickly responded. "It helped burn the fuel more efficiently and completely, thereby improving both gas mileage and acceleration."

"That certainly is a big 'so what' for any automobile manufacturer."

"It really is, especially with Corvettes and other high-performance vehicles with big engines," Josh agreed. "That's why I can't figure out why I'm not rich yet." With that, Josh himself led the laughter.

As much as Rachel enjoyed the story—and the humor—she was getting a tad impatient. She had a packed workday ahead of her. "Can we hear about the *R* in HORSE?"

"Of course. The *R* represents 'Relevant information or data.' This is where you present the essential information that supports your 'so what.' That information could include things such as research findings and test results. It also might include what human and technological resources could be required to achieve the desired end.

"Whatever outcome you're seeking, you must build your case.

"This usually involves incorporating facts, data, scientific research, or the opinions or endorsements of knowledgeable, informed people. It can also involve news reports or documentaries—but beware of 'fake news.'

"Of course, a part of the solution can revolve around asking the right questions of your audience.

"And, yes, it can even involve an emotional appeal. Just proceed with caution on this one. There is always a chance that kind of approach could come off as hokey or contrived."

Josh piped up. "I get that. As you know, even though I came close to crying during Rachel's LLS presentation, I am not overflowing with emotion. That approach would probably backfire on me because it would not be authentic."

"Could be," Ron replied with a warm smile.

"Aw, don't sell yourself short, Josh," Rachel said encouragingly. Then she added, "I'm sorry, Ron. Please continue."

"Okay. The *S* in HORSE tells you to 'Summarize the key point or points.' Sometimes in shorter presentations or with shorter agenda items, this can be optional. I have witnessed—and even been a part of—presentations where the event is running long, and the time allotted for a presentation is limited. As a result, on the fly, the speaker needs to decide what to cut. The summary is something that often could be eliminated."

"So, you're saying, yet again," Rachel said, "that presenters need to be prepared to make last-minute changes . . . to be adaptable?"

"Exactly," Ron agreed. "And, as you already know, one of those changes often involves the length of time you have available. Another change could be that the key decision maker is unable to attend, and you're suddenly addressing an unanticipated audience. This requires some fast thinking. You may have to rethink your HORSE."

Rachel pressed on. "How about the *E*?"

"The *E* represents 'Ease into your next *H*.' That means to highlight the point of your next agenda item or ease to your close. Create a Transition Statement or use your agenda as a transition slide."

"Can you explain that in more detail?" Josh queried.

Ron thought for a moment. "Okay, do you recall when Rachel said that her agenda was 'Past, Present, and Future' in her presentation?"

"Yes, I do."

"Here's what this means. Because she is offering three distinct pieces, I think it makes sense for her to have a HORSE in each of the three agenda items. And it also makes sense to *ease* into the sections as she starts with the next H."

"I can do that," Rachel agreed.

"Great! I think it will help with your overall flow and will help you remember to include all your points."

Ron then handed Josh and Rachel a packet that summarized how to create a presentation agenda, along with how to write a HORSE for each agenda item. "If you turn to page two of this handout, you'll see a graphic that you can use to remind yourself of the key points of HORSE."

Rachel and Josh flipped their pages.

FORMULA FOR PRESENTATION SUCCESS:

Tell them . . . Agenda with a concise body message

Body: The main points with transitions (each main point needs a HORSE)
H – Highlight the main point (hottest topic starts)
O – Okay, so what?
R – Relevant information/data
S – Summarize the point (optional)
E – Ease to your next *H* or finish strong

"Rachel, Josh, do you have any questions as we wrap up this session?"

Josh said, "I do have one question. How would we ever use the HORSE in an informal presentation?"

"That is a valid question," Ron responded. "Think about preparing for an important meeting or interview. Rachel could use the same agenda and organize her thoughts using the HORSE acronym around each of her agenda items—Past, Present, and Future. If she was leading the meeting, she could facilitate highlighting the main point of each agenda item, being clear on 'Okay, so what,' providing relevant data, and easing to the next point or close. I use the HORSE for any important meeting I'm leading or facilitating because it is also a tool to have a clear, productive meeting."

"Thank you," Josh replied. "There's just a lot for me to think about."

"Same here," Rachel concurred.

Ron said, "Once you start to use the HORSE to create a clear body message in any presentation or communication, it will become second nature—just like riding a horse! Okay, that's it for today. See you next week."

TAKE A MOMENT . . .

Think about your next likely (or possible) presentation or interview:

1. What is the best way to organize your agenda? In other words, outline the main points/topic areas in your agenda.

_____

_____

_____

_____

2. Now outline the HORSE for each of your main agenda items. H = Highlight the point (hottest topic starts); O = Okay, so what?; R = Relevant information/data; S = Summarize the point (optional for shorter agenda items); and E = Ease to next H or to your close.

_____

_____

_____

_____

3. Imagine that you are competing for a significant promotion or applying for a new job or even trying to get investors to invest in your business. How would you use HORSE in how you present yourself?

_____

_____

_____

_____

12

Finish Strong and Summarize

RON BEGAN THIS latest session on effective presentations with a question.

"Have you ever gone to—or taken some kids to—a fireworks display, and nothing special happens at the end of the show? No big finish? No finale? You get in your car or board the train to go home, and the big thought on your mind is *Well, that sure was a disappointment. I expected more.*

"Just as you, your family members, and other viewers expected a big finish, so the people in the audience for your presentation expect to leave with a thought in their minds: *I get it!* or *That's fantastic* or *Thank you.*

"Finishing Strong or ending with a 'Fireworks Close' to your presentation ideally should include a call to action. This is where you come back to the desired outcome you expressed in your Executive Summary and ask your audience to give you what you asked for, such as a decision, approval to go to a next step, and so on.

"Personally, I prefer the phrase 'Finish Strong' to 'Fireworks Close,' and the reason goes back to my story about the flashy presenter who bombed in Australia. It's important to be aware of cultural differences when traveling and presenting abroad. It's also important to consider regional differences within your own country. Finish Strong is a better descriptor of how to best close a presentation that can be used across different cultures. In fact, when we did the APPS program for our Australia office, the participants confirmed they much preferred Finish Strong over Fireworks Close.

"The closing is your final opportunity to make your magic. There is nothing more important than your attention-getting opening to capture your audience's attention during your presentation. However, it is your close that drives their action after your presentation has been completed. With this being what they remember, your closing should include a recap of your main points.

"Ask yourself these questions when preparing the close of your presentation:

"First, 'After my presentation, what will they believe that is different?'

"Second, 'After my presentation, what action will the audience take that is different?'

"Third, 'After my presentation, what new information will they know that is different from what they knew or believed going in?'

"In addition to summarizing your main points, there are several other ways to end your presentation by Finishing Strong.

"For example, a powerful technique when finishing an in-person presentation is to physically move toward the audience just as you are making your closing statements. This will add emphasis to what you are saying, and it's a clear *presence* technique.

"As in the opening, time here is of the essence. Announce your close. How do you announce it? Hopefully, *not* by saying, 'In closing, I'd like to . . .' What you want to do is summarize and call them to action. If you have time to take questions, this is where you do that. Remember the advice of President Franklin Roosevelt: 'Be brief, be sincere, be seated.'"

Rachel desperately scribbled this information in her notebook, trying to keep up.

"Here are some proven closing techniques. In many ways, they mirror the 'attention-getting opening' strategies.

"First, you could close with a quote: A powerful, relevant quote that is practiced and delivered with confidence can add the perfect crescendo to your presentation.

"Second, you could conclude with a pertinent story to captivate your audience. Dramatic, humorous, surprising, or allegorical stories leave a lasting impression. If you are using a story and delivering a presentation using slides, I highly recommend having a black blank on a slide as you tell your story so all eyes are on you and the audience has nowhere else to look. It helps them listen to you. Alternatively, you can choose some powerful large images to support your story.

"A possible fitting example could be Rachel's story on how she has raised money for lymphoma and leukemia and watched her friend battle this awful disease.

"Third, you could close by emphasizing or completing an earlier point: Answer a question that you asked earlier in your presentation, or repeat a particularly important point. This is an excellent way to reinforce your message. Repetition can be overdone. The opposite can also be true. Sometimes, repetition can't be overemphasized. Based on the importance of something, it may well be worth repeating a number of times.

"Fourth, you could close with a question or a startling statistic: Close with a question or possibly a series of questions with appropriate pauses in between. Many of those in the audience want to participate in the presentation experience. By asking questions, and allowing a pause for time to reflect, you will engage the audience in your programming thought pattern. I don't know if you've ever heard this, but Mark Twain is quoted as advising, 'The right word may be effective, but no word was ever as effective as a rightly timed pause.'

"Fifth, you can close with a powerful image or series of images. If you are sure a video will work, then it can also be powerful to close with a video.

"Finally, you can close with a challenge. If you want the members of your audience to take action, now is the time to specifically indicate that.

"The audience must clearly understand what you want them to do. Make your recommendation to them extremely clear!

"To set up the action you want them to take, a memorable quote is often useful. You most likely are familiar with these often-used quotations: 'No one else can make you feel inferior without your consent.'

'And so, my fellow Americans, ask not what your country can do for you—ask what you can do for your country.'

"There are vast resources of quotes and statements that can even be modified to fit your specific needs. I suggest that you go online and look for BrainyQuote. Then, start typing the name of your favorite people into the search line. You might get hooked on this site."

"I *have* used it!" Josh chimed in. "And you're right. I *did* get hooked! I was looking for inspiring quotes from astronauts, rocket scientists, and people such as Richard Branson. He's one of my personal innovation heroes."

"That's interesting, Josh. There are obviously dimensions to you that we know nothing about," Ron commented.

"You have *no* idea," Josh replied. "But I'm working on my Authentic Brand Statement, and that will reveal more."

"Can't wait, Josh!" Rachel interjected, hoping her attempt at humor wasn't missed. "Meanwhile, can we all get back on topic while your mind is somewhere off in the clouds? I have another busy day ahead."

Ron quickly agreed. "Great idea, Rachel! I have a full day ahead of me, too. 'Do, hear, see, go.' In addition to finding the best ways to end your presentation, there are also a few things you should avoid.

"First, avoid abrupt closings. Ease into the closing so that the audience is aware that it is coming. Be sure to summarize your key points and emphasize the actions to be taken.

"Second, avoid the endless closing. Do not go over in your allotted time, and do not tease the audience with a false close only to continue with additional information. Chances are that the audience has probably already stopped listening. Attention spans are getting shorter and shorter, thanks, in part, to sound bites on social media.

"If at all possible, don't read your close. Based on the importance of this segment, it is very important to have it prepared in such a way that notes are not necessary.

"Your goal, of course, is to send your audience on their way, all fired up."

"It worked for me!" Rachel immediately affirmed. "I'm all fired up!"

"I think I get it." It was the best Josh could muster. "See you all next week."

TAKE A MOMENT . . .

Think about your next likely (or possible) presentation or interview:

1. What might be a great way to Finish Strong at the end of your next presentation?

_____

_____

_____

2. What are some of your favorite quotes or stories that you could use to end some of your presentations?

_____

_____

_____

13

Practice Makes Better

AS WAS NOW typical and expected of these meetings, this one began exactly on time.

But, this week, Ron had a bit of a surprise for his protégés.

"Today, I've invited Victoria to handle the introduction of new material. I view her as an authority on the significance of practice."

"I think that's a great idea," Rachel said. "Please don't take me wrong, Ron. It's not that we're tired of learning from you. But I think a female perspective on presence and presentation skills would be meaningful . . . especially to me. After all, women now make up almost 50 percent of our workforce, by some estimates. And that percentage appears to be growing."[1]

"If that's true," Josh interjected, "it's important that we learn how to present effectively to both men and women so we hit the right points."

Ron instantly agreed. "Great point, Josh."

"In any case, one thing is a sure bet," Victoria added. "Both men and women value effective authentic presence, as well as careful, skilled presentation. And that is why I am here today.

---

1   US Department of Labor, "12 Stats about Working Women," March 1, 2017, https://blog.dol.gov/2017/03/01/12-stats-about-working-women.

"Think for a moment about great athletes, great musicians, or great anythings. They did not become great solely through natural abilities. At some point, becoming great involves practice, and that is our topic today.

"As I'm sure you already know, *preparation is key*. But preparation is more than the *content* of your presentation. You can have all the facts, details, and supporting data available, but if you don't deliver it properly, your message won't achieve the results you desire.

"For that reason, *practice is the second key*. In fact, it is an essential part of preparation."

"That makes sense to me," Rachel said.

Josh nodded.

Victoria smiled. "Good! But how do you effectively practice your presentation?"

"No clue," Josh admitted.

Victoria continued, "I believe there are three ways to practice.

"The first way is to deliver your presentation in front of a mirror, ideally a full-length mirror. The inherent problem with that is that we all tend to focus on what we want to see. And we often get so caught up in real time that we miss important clues.

"The second way is to find a captive audience, usually family or friends. Or you could practice with each other, or other peers. There's a problem there, too, and that's that your listeners will likely want to avoid upsetting you, so they may not be totally honest. They may not tell you the truth."

Ron interrupted. "I don't think that would be true with Josh and Rachel, though. They might tend to be too honest . . . to the point of being brutal."

They all laughed. "Funny, Ron!" Rachel said.

Victoria completed her three ways to practice by sharing: "The third way is to use video to record your presentation rehearsal. Your smartphone can undoubtedly do this, or do a Zoom or Webex meeting and video yourself. I personally think that a full-length view is best. And frame a wide angle to capture any movements from side to side. The video recording of both practice and final presentations is something they do in the official APPS course, because participants learn so much about themselves through seeing themselves on video."

"So, practice makes perfect?" Josh asked.

"No, not really," Victoria responded. "'Practice makes permanent or better.' Every time we do something, we improve . . . little by little. That's our reasonable expectation."

"Makes sense," both candidates agreed.

"One more major point. As you watch your videos, you'll want to make note of three important things:

"First, your *facial expressions*. Don't scowl or frown. Make sure you are pleasant to look at. This is not a game of *Angry Birds* or an episode of *Grumpy Cat*.

"Second, your *hand gestures*. Are they natural or overly restrained? Above all, don't point at your audience. That would make you look as though you're shooting or scolding them. I know that's a tiny point, but you certainly don't want to appear hostile. When you are not using your hands for emphasis, then let them rest at your sides. I see so many people rest their hands over their solar plexus or in front of their chest or at their pelvis or even behind them, which I find distracting.

"Third, your *use of the podium* . . . or stage. How do you move around in the space allotted to you? I always suggest that you try to practice in a space that is roughly the same size area that you will have when you do your actual presentation. That's why you want to frame your video using a wider angle than you may think is correct.

"If you're doing a virtual presentation, consider having a professional background. Please don't do a virtual presentation on your bed; instead have a blank wall or a wall with a nice picture, or better yet, develop a virtual background in Zoom, Webex, or Teams. Whenever I do a Zoom presentation, I have our company logo as my background or at least *in* my background. Also, when presenting virtually, remember to make eye contact with your camera, not the small videos of audience members, or it will look like you're looking down instead of at your audience.

"One more important tip. Learn how to *time yourself*. You can use a watch for a close-enough timing if your smartphone is busy filming you.

"Many, if not most, of your presentations will involve time limits. It's vital that you adhere to those limits. On the other hand, don't expand your material to fill the allotted time, unless you really have something important to say. Make every minute—every second—count. Also, if your time is cut at the last minute, use the time you do have to present your Executive Summary. That's where you should have clearly organized all of your key points. I have known presenters who have gotten a yes from their audience by only showing that one Executive Summary slide. If that happens to you, be grateful, and don't feel like you have to finish your presentation. Simply say, 'Thank you for your time and your decision,' and exit. Consider it a great victory if you get a yes on your Executive Summary alone."

Victoria concluded with "I highly recommend that between now and your final presentation, you video record yourself giving your intended final presentation. Get a colleague to review it with you, someone you trust and who will give you direct and honest feedback. Then record yourself one more time and review again. I have found that the third time you give a presentation is the best—so practice at least twice before you give your final presentation to Ron and me."

With that, Josh thanked her, and both he and Rachel stood up to leave.

"Hold on one moment, please," Ron interrupted. "We still have time remaining in our hour together, and now that we have just about completed the *your presentation* part of The Authenticity Code™, I want to address one more important topic."

TAKE A MOMENT . . .

1. If you decide to practice your next presentation, what method will you use?

_____

_____

_____

_____

2. Who will you choose to watch, review, or evaluate your practice presentation?

_____

_____

_____

_____

14

Expressing Your Authentic Image

EVERYONE RETURNED TO their seats, and Josh let out a sigh. "I know that we have discussed some of this before," Ron began, "but we need to discuss the matter of expressing your authentic image, especially as it relates to also respecting the culture of your workplace. The specifics we will consider include etiquette and dressing for your target audience. Your authentic image is a big part of the *your presence* part of The Authenticity Code™. And as we all know, it can make or break a presentation or job interview."

Josh responded, "We sure *have* discussed it before. After our first presentation, you basically told me that I was a walking disaster. You criticized my jeans, my shirt, and my shoes. In fact, I felt like you were picking on me."

"I'm sorry," Ron shot back. "I really wasn't. I just wanted to let you know that these things are important."

Rachel chimed in, "I agree with Ron, Josh. The truth is, I felt a little picked on, too. I now know that the '60s hippie look isn't right for our company. We tend to be 'classic professional.'"

"You're right, Rachel," Ron quickly added. "The good news is, there are successful companies out there that may better fit you both. They care more about your knowledge and skills than your wardrobe. They're more into what's in your mind than what's in your closet."

Josh grinned as he said, "That's good to know!"

Without any hesitation, Rachel said, "I'm happy here. I'll 'play the game' any way I am expected to. And, yes, I know it's not a game. I'm being authentic here. I authentically want to advance my career at World Wide Synergistics, because I'm making an authentic choice as to both my audience and our culture."

"Good to know that," Ron observed. "As I told you before, *you* are the only one who can choose your audience. If you want to work for Disney, the audience you are choosing will be families, many with young children.

"When you work here, or in most Fortune 500 companies, you are choosing to dress for a corporate environment. That means you are being authentic, given your choices. Of course, there are companies out there that tend to be, shall we say, looser in the image expectations. And some of them are even top tier in their industries."

"I may prefer those top-tier companies, I guess," Josh muttered to Rachel.

Ron and Victoria both rolled their eyes, having heard the comment. Josh noticed but wasn't sure he really cared.

"May I add something, please?" Victoria asked.

"Of course. Yes," Ron said.

"I believe that basic etiquette is also important, especially in business meetings involving lunch, dinner, or receptions. By that, I mean five simple things.

"First, watch the alcohol consumption. An extra beer or three may be fine at a ball game with friends, but it's not okay at most business events.

And remember, it's not okay to drive if you have had those extra beers. Try to keep alcohol consumption for a work event to one or two beverages.

"Second, learn how to handle hors d'oeuvres and respond to greetings from other attendees, too. This might require some practice. If shaking hands is an accepted business practice in the company culture or international culture, you don't want to shake hands with sticky fingers or, more importantly, if you are a bit under the weather."

Rachel wrinkled her nose. "Yuck! It's happened to me."

Victoria smiled knowingly. "Third, know what fork or knife or spoon to use when. It can be daunting, with such a variety of tableware. Bread knife, salad fork, dessert fork. It can go on and on. I always recommend the acronym BMW. Bread plate goes on the left, meal plate in the middle, wine and water glasses on the right. I am handing you a diagram so you know your place settings. And when it comes to which item of flatware to use first or second, you generally will begin the meal with the pieces farthest from the center plate. In other words, on the *outside*. Believe it or not, how you wine and dine can really impact whether you get the job you want or close the deal you most desire. And how you treat your waitstaff is often a reflection of how you treat others in general.

"Here is a graphic I use when I do a presentation on table settings and etiquette. Of course, this is the typical table setting for a formal dinner. Sometimes, when steak is served, there also may be a serrated steak knife.

"Fourth, know how to signal to the waitstaff that you have finished. Rather than saying, 'Woudja take my plate outta here? I'm done,' simply cross your knife and fork in the middle of the plate. And, no, your napkin should not be refolded!

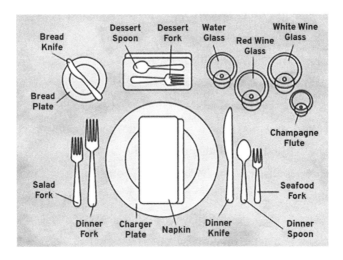

A Key to a Formal Place Setting

"Finally, know when to make your exit—never before the presentation or main feature. Don't be the first one to leave . . . or the last one, either."

Josh asked, "Are you going to teach us all of that now?"

"Goodness no," Victoria responded. "It's covered in detail in Inside-Out Learning's in person APPS program. They teach it in a really fun way as the program participants are all having dinner together. You will really enjoy the etiquette dinner when you take the course."

Ron concluded the meeting. "I think your attention spans are waning. Time to tackle the rest of the day. See you in a week. We'll be discussing the visual aspects of your presentations—specifically charts, slides, or videos, as well as props. They can be truly effective ways to communicate!"

TAKE A MOMENT . . .

1. Are you comfortable in a formal business dinner setting? If so, why? If not, why not? Remember to review the place setting picture on page 104 before you attend your next formal dinner.

    _____

    _____

    _____

    _____

2. Think about an upcoming presentation you have, what is the best way to dress for your authentically chosen target audience? What will you plan to wear?

    _____

    _____

    _____

    _____

15

Using Nonverbal Communication Effectively

THE FOLLOWING MONDAY, Rachel buzzed with anticipation for her next meeting with Ron—and with Josh, of course!

This is so exciting, she thought as she took her seat in Ron's office. *I'm learning so much! I've always loved visual presentations. Maybe that's why I enjoy movies and documentaries so much!*

Josh, who found himself more rejuvenated and involved, had his own thoughts: *Awesome! Another meeting. Maybe today is the day I'll figure out how to become "authentic."*

Ron entered the office with no fanfare. (He never really needed or demanded it.)

Victoria surprised everyone by showing up, too, because she had sent an email saying she could not make it to this meeting due to a schedule conflict. "I *had* to be here, so I changed my schedule! I'm learning a lot myself."

Ron didn't waste any time getting to the point of the meeting.

"Have either of you ever used Microsoft PowerPoint or Apple Keynote —or any similar software—in a presentation? To anyone? At any time?" he asked them.

Rachel shook her head. "Yes, I have. But I'm still a novice," she reluctantly admitted.

"I have," Josh volunteered.

Sudden silence.

"And?" Ron said, ending the ensuing discomfort, he hoped.

"Well, I *have* used it, a lot," Josh responded, "and it didn't go well. I was attempting to train the people in my department about how to write effective and complete user manuals on our products. They just sat there, dumbfounded, like a massive, inert collection of speed bumps."

"I'm sorry to hear that," Ron replied.

Victoria interjected, "Ron, you have always used presentation software as effectively as anyone I know. Would you be willing to share your 'deepest, darkest secrets' with your protégés?"

Josh laughed.

He wasn't alone. Everyone chuckled!

Ron was ready! "Of course I would. But my secrets are not that deep or dark. I've learned them all by watching others do it correctly. I love watching TED talks in my rare free time."

Rachel, Josh, and even Victoria prepared to take notes. *No one can afford to stop learning . . . ever!* Victoria thought as she fired up her tablet.

"Okay," Ron began. "The very *first* thing is BLUF, 'bottom line up front.' Your projector—your charts, slides, or whatever visuals you use—is *not* your presentation. Same thing with any props you choose to employ. Same thing with the gestures you use. The truth is *you* are the *presentation.* Everything else is there to support your ideas, to make your point convincingly and memorably. To get your audience to 'ride your HORSE,' so to speak. To lead them to the point of decision or buy-in."

"That makes sense to me," Rachel commented.

"And I thought that's exactly what I did every time," Josh said, almost in self-defense.

Ron continued: "It's more than *what* you do; it's *how* you do it."

Victoria added, "Please listen to Ron! He knows what he's talking about!"

"We are listening," Rachel and Josh affirmed in unison.

"Great!" Ron replied. "This information is crucial to your success. I'm sorry that there aren't appropriate handouts in the packets I gave you initially, but much of this is—or *should* be—commonsense information. So we can simply talk about it in this setting."

The "students" both agreed, as did Victoria.

"Your visuals, charts, and slides are part of your nonverbal communication. In other words, your visuals are a reflection of who you are. Clear visuals equal a clear you. The basic truth is a chart or slide needs to be *readable* if it is to be *useful*.

"There are a number of factors that contribute to readability: The first is the typestyle, or font, that you choose to use. Avoid script fonts or handwritten fonts or anything frilly.

"There have been numerous studies done on this topic. The findings are that of the current popular fonts, Arial is one of the most readable. There are other great fonts, of course, but Arial is available in a wide range of weights . . . including Narrow, Regular, Bold, and Black.

"The second big point is the *background color* you choose. Naturally, there must be sufficient *contrast* between the font color and the background color. And, remember, many people—mostly men—are color-blind."

At this point, Rachel raised her hand.

"Yes, Rachel. Do you have a question?"

"I do. You never mentioned the size of the type. Is size important?"

With that, Josh burst out in uproarious laughter and said, "Not for an aspiring engineer. We prefer small type, because we always have a lot to say."

"You sure had me fooled, Josh, because you haven't said all that much in our sessions," Ron observed. Then, he continued, "Good question, Rachel. The purpose of every visual is to enhance understanding for your intended audience. Research has shown that you only have three to five seconds to convey your message in each point you make on a slide. Therefore, bigger type will always result in fewer words, and I recommend a minimum of 21-point font. I have seen slides packed with so many tiny words that trying to take it all in is much like trying to read the front page of your Sunday newspaper from a distance of 75 feet."

"Newspapers still exist?" Josh posed, in another attempt to inject humor.

"They may not exist in *your* world, but they still exist in *mine*," Ron countered, lightheartedly. "The point is, keep it simple and direct, or you risk losing your audience.

"Your presentation software, whether PowerPoint, Keynote, Prezi, or something else, will give you many options as to the manipulation of type and images.

"*Transitions* are another consideration, especially if you want to come off as completely professional. One of my favorite ways to transition to the next point is to use the PowerPoint animation Appear.

"You don't want your transitions to be overly flashy or distracting, so most practitioners recommend Appear, where the new point quickly and clearly appears with each click of your presentation clicker. Another technique I use is, as a new point appears, I gray out the previous points and use Appear animation to bring the next point on in black font. These techniques help you maintain the focus of your audience on your current, most recent point, discouraging them from reading ahead and not listening to you."

"Wow!" Josh replied. "That sure makes sense to me. I really appreciate these tips, Ron. By your standards, the last slide presentation I did was a complete mess. I think I used eight-point font, and there was no white space on my slides. Just lots of words, all at once."

"Thanks, Josh. That's why this part of The Authenticity Code™ is actually *your presence.* Cluttered visuals communicate a cluttered you. Yes, your audience can assume that if your visuals are cluttered, then your head and thinking and presence are also cluttered. They think you are dependent on your slides and not confident in what you know. I have a few more important tips; a couple of them involve the use of images along with type.

"First, the best practice is to place the image on the left side of the slide and place the type on the right side. We are visual beings, and the brain remembers the image first, which helps in making your point.

"A second tip is to have any people who are in the image facing to the right, or toward the type. This helps draw your viewers' attention toward the words, instead of away from them. If the people in your slide are staring off into space, chances are really good that the viewers will do that, too."

At this point, Josh politely raised his hand. "I have a question that may appear to be stupid. I think I already know the answer, but I still have to ask it."

Ron chuckled. "Please continue, Josh."

"Okay, here goes. Is there some underlying reason why you—and so many presenters—place an emphasis on visuals, slides, and charts?"

Ron smiled. "That's not a stupid question at all, Josh. And I'm really glad you asked it.

"Very simply, visuals, slides, or charts should be an important part of your presentation, because most learning takes place on the visual level and not on the auditory level.

"Consider these obvious facts:

"First, we live in a visual world. We watch TV. We go to the movies. We enjoy art galleries. Many of us express ourselves visually, whether it's through painting or photography, dance, or even the way we dress."

"Yeah, I tried expressing myself through the dressing thing. It bombed," Josh observed.

Everyone laughed.

Ron regained his composure and marched onward.

"Think about the first book you enjoyed as a child. Chances are it was a picture book. Yes, I realize that Dr. Seuss's books also include words, and when she was much younger, my daughter's favorite book was *Pat the Bunny*, which also offered a great tactile learning experience.

"The fact is, 75 percent of everything we know today, we learned visually. Studies show that 90 percent of all information that comes into our brains is visual.

"Even more interesting is research from the University of Minnesota, the University of Arizona, and 3M—the manufacturing company—that shows our brains absorb images 60,000 times faster than words."

"That's remarkable!" Rachel added.

"I believe that," Josh piped in. "That's why I always include so many pictures and drawings in our product manuals and sales literature."

"I'm aware that you do that, Josh," Ron said. "That's a big reason why you're one of two finalists for this position."

"Thank you," Josh replied as Rachel muttered, "Well, that sure makes *me* feel special."

"Trust me, Rachel. You *are* special," Ron pointed out. "We can't all have the same interests, education, skills, and goals. We are unique. *You* are unique!"

"Thank you," she replied timidly. "I didn't mean to come across as negative."

"I'm sure," Victoria said. "From what I've learned about you so far, that would have been out of character for you."

Ron wrapped up the meeting. "I have an assignment for both of you to do by our next meeting. I would like you to prepare a five-minute presentation that uses visuals. It can be on any subject you choose, just so long as it is not focused on the promotion you're seeking. That will come later, of course."

"*Any* topic?" Josh asked.

"Exactly. Just make sure that you use visuals. We want to see what you've learned. Oh, and do *not* exceed the five-minute time limit, under any circumstances. If you apply what I have taught today, you will notice one very important thing—*you become the presentation.* Your slides are not your presentation. Your slides simply support you as the presenter. So many presenters read their slides and are dependent on them. The key is to trust that *you are the presentation.* And remember when you realize you *are* the presentation, you have achieved the art of success. See you next week."

TAKE A MOMENT . . .

1. Have you ever used a visual presentation program? If so, which one(s)?

_____

_____

_____

_____

2. When you start to write your next presentation, challenge yourself to apply the tips provided in this chapter.

_____

_____

_____

_____

16

The Second "Battle Round"

RACHEL AND JOSH arrived at the conference room for the meeting, both convinced that they had this simple assignment nailed. They each realized that even though this was not the final presentation on why they should get the promotion, they were still competing. How they performed in this presentation would provide Ron and Victoria more information on how they would perform as the associate director of Sales.

Rachel spent the better part of the weekend preparing her visuals, and although she did not follow every guideline Ron shared, she thought her visuals were really impactful. However, she did not get a lot of time to practice. Over the weekend, as Josh was working on his latest invention, he had an idea about how a childhood experience could be a great opening for his presentation. Being into brevity, he wrote only one slide, yet he did practice how to best tell his story. For the first time in a long time, Josh started to feel more confident, because he was discovering more and more about his authentic self and his natural gift for storytelling.

It may have been due to his military background, but "Ron's Rules and Regulations" seemed to state "ladies first," so he asked Rachel to take the podium to start the meeting.

She connected her laptop to the digital screen and tapped on the microphone while saying the typical, "Testing, one, two." Then she mumbled, "Volume is kinda low. I guess I'll have to talk louder."

In an attempt to be cute or funny, Josh loudly responded, "WHAT?"

Rachel's reaction was to glare at him.

She put her first slide on the screen. It said, "THE BATTLE AGAINST LEUKEMIA AND LYMPHOMA: What the Leukemia and Lymphoma Society Is Doing Today to Win This Battle for Tomorrow."

After she had given her "audience" plenty of time to read the words, she began speaking: "As you can tell, my presentation is about the tragedy of this terrible, often fatal disease.

"I am giving this presentation in honor of Julia, my college sorority sister who fought this battle herself. Thankfully, she survived and is doing well today! As a matter of fact, she changed her field of study to ultimately earn her bachelor of science in nursing."

Josh applauded.

Rachel then clicked the remote to change to the next slide. Except nothing happened. She clicked again. "Oops, I must have dead batteries." Undaunted, she walked over to her laptop and pushed the appropriate button.

"Better," she said as the second slide appeared. Except it wasn't better. It was a mishmash of tiny words in a fancy script font and graphics. "Wow!" she hastily observed. "It sure looked better at home."

What did the second slide say? No one was really sure, but the distracted audience listened to Rachel as she explained the contents. Something about the effects of the disease. Something about the statistics of whom it affects. Something about the society (LLS). Something about research. Something about the future. Something about how to give to LLS. Yes, it was *truly something*!

Rachel ended her presentation with "Thank you! That's all." And she returned to her seat.

Ron politely said, "Thank you, Rachel." Then he added, "Okay, Josh. You're up."

Josh went to the side of the room and retrieved some sort of pedestal with an object on top, all covered by a black cloth. He then moved it all to a table near center stage.

"What on earth is going on?" Victoria whispered to Ron. Ron shrugged.

Since Josh knew that technology could fail anyone, he pulled out a second remote control and clicked on it. Sure enough, his first graphic appeared on the screen. It said, "JOSHUA ARMSTRONG'S FIRST SCIENTIFIC DISCOVERY: Age 8."

He began: "When I was seven, my family lived in Brooklyn, New York, in an area called Bay Ridge, near the Verrazzano-Narrows Bridge. One day my dad came home from the plant, and he and my mom told me that I was going to have a baby brother or sister. I was excited, but our house was small, and we did not have a lot of money, so I wondered where they were going to put this thing when it showed up.

"That question was answered one day when a big yellow machine showed up and began digging. 'We're adding on to the house to make room for the baby—and maybe your grandma, too,' my parents said. Turns out Grandma paid for the addition so she could live with us and not be so lonely.

"I watched as the big yellow machine dug and dug. On the second day of digging, they uncovered something, and I immediately made it mine.

"I have it with me today. It's under this cloth covering. And it was my first-ever scientific discovery."

With great dramatic flourish, Josh yanked the cloth away, revealing

. . . a large, gray, smooth, egg-shaped rock! The audience of three was *stunned*! They *could* have been, anyway.

Josh continued: "This, folks, is a genuine prehistoric *dinosaur egg!* It's probably 100 million years old if it's a day!"

Chuckles rippled through the rapt tiny audience.

"Hark! I believe I hear a smattering of laughter. You say you don't believe me? To that, I submit this challenge: Prove me wrong."[2]

On his way back to his seat, Josh hit a button on his remote control that turned the screen to black. At the same time, he enjoyed as much thunderous applause as a crowd of three could provide.

Rachel and Josh sat in silent anticipation as Ron and Victoria continued to scribble notes.

After a pause that seemed to last forever, Ron asked for Victoria's notes and stepped up to the podium. He placed both sets of notes on the lectern and began as gently as he could.

"Rachel, lucky you! You're first.

"I must have rushed through our last class. Or maybe my ability to make things clear is failing fast.

"I have to say that, again, I was really interested in your topic. I expected this presentation to be much stronger than your first Executive Summary presentation. When I was 19, my 16-year-old cousin died of leukemia. This was a long time ago, and medical research had not made all the recent advances that save lives today."

"I'm sorry," Rachel offered.

---

2   The story about the "Dinosaur Egg Rock" was adapted from original material first presented at the 2003 Toastmasters Regional Speech Contest (semifinal round for the World Championship of Public Speaking) in Lubbock, Texas, by Michael Desiderio, MBA and member of Dobson Ranch Toastmasters in Mesa, Arizona. Mr. Desiderio is currently the executive director of the EMBA Council, a global association of business schools that offer executive MBA programs. Mr. Desiderio has the opportunity to speak to various groups around the globe annually. He credits his still-active participation in Toastmasters for the ability to entertain and educate audiences.

THE SECOND "BATTLE ROUND"

Ron smiled, sadness visible in his eyes.

"The thing is, Rachel, I thought I told you these key things: easy-to-read type, very few keywords, and a contrasting background color. Instead, your chosen type was a fancy script font—almost like poor handwriting—you had too many words on your first slide, and your second slide was confusing and impossible to read. It had too many points, the type was too small, and your key ideas would have been better served with several additional slides—one for each main point. If I failed to tell you those things, or emphasize them adequately, I am truly sorry."

Rachel responded, "I *do* recall you saying those things. I'm sorry, Ron. I'll do better next time. I promise."

"Thank you, Rachel," Ron said as he captured her gaze. "There are two more helpful points I would like to offer you. First, when you initially got up in front, your remote control didn't work. Yes, it could have been weak batteries. But an experienced presenter needs to check all of the technical aspects beforehand—in your case, the remote, as well as the sound level. To be fair, in many presentations, you will have the advantage of a technical support team, so it would be less of a concern.

"But there is an even greater concern. I told you that color-blindness is quite common, particularly with men. What I didn't tell you is that I am color-blind. Maybe I should have mentioned that fact, but if you put red type on a green background, I'm sure I missed it.

"So my summary, Rachel, is that you had an interesting topic, it was both personal and important, but you need to perfect your overall presentation skills."

"Thank you, Ron. That is something I really desire to do."

"Wonderful! Josh, you're next."

"Yes, sir."

"Josh, I really think you get this!"

"That could be due to the fact that it is largely about technology," Josh suggested.

"Could be. But preparation was also involved. First, you got up there with a working remote control.

"Second, you must have paid attention in all of our previous sessions. You used few words on your only slide.

"Third, you used a creative prop. It was relevant to your presentation and not just clever for the sake of being clever.

"Fourth, you had a great attention-getting opening. I could even picture the 'big yellow machine' carving into your yard. I missed telling you both one very significant point about attention-getting openings; that's the element of *mystery* or *surprise*. You did that beautifully! You also went to a black slide at the end. That was a great idea. When you use a black blank, the audience's complete attention is on you! I often recommend this technique when a presenter is telling a story because then the audience has nowhere else to focus except on the presenter's story.

"Finally, you were brief, got to the point, and left the podium. My only unanswered question: Did you end up with a baby brother or a baby sister?"

"Neither! I ended up with a baby dinosaur! Just kidding. It was a sister, and she is now a cellist with the New York Philharmonic. I love her with all my heart!"

"That's wonderful! But I have a question for both of you . . . then I'll respond.

"Here's the question: Could you have made your presentations effectively without slides or charts? Of *course* you could have. Rachel, your presentation might have been more genuine and heartfelt without them. And, Josh, you only used one slide. Your words were captivating enough. Yet, I think you benefitted from the rock prop.

"Always remember, the secret to the art of success is when you realize and believe that *you are the presentation*, not your slides!"

Victoria added, "Great point, Ron! One more point: I think both of you can be better than your past best in your final presentation by following the formula for presentation success that Ron taught you. Remember the five steps and demonstrate them in your final presentation. While the secret to the art of success is realizing that *you are* the presentation, the secret to the science of success is following The Authenticity Code™ formula and guidelines we have given you on your presence, your audience, and your presentation."

Josh said, "Thank you for that reminder, Victoria. If I remember correctly, step one is know your audience, step two is attention-getting opening, step three is Executive Summary, step four is agenda with clear body message—HORSE—and step five is Finish Strong. You're right. I could have done a better job on the Executive Summary, agenda, and using the HORSE."

"Great insight," Victoria added. "However, you absolutely nailed knowing your audience, the attention-getting opening, the use of props and visuals, and Finishing Strong. You also demonstrated the art of success—that you *are* the presentation!"

"Thanks so much for your feedback." Josh blushed.

Ron concluded the meeting. "This was a practice session; learn from it, and use the feedback, as Victoria said, to 'be better than your past best' in your final presentation. Please bring the packets that I gave you at the first meeting to our next meeting. We have to cover some vital material about authentic presence qualities."

TAKE A MOMENT . . .

1. Can you think of any presenters you've seen who have done it right?

_____

_____

_____

_____

2. What specific things did the presenters do that you think were good/ effective?

_____

_____

_____

_____

3. The next time you do a high stakes presentation, videotape yourself on your phone and review with yourself or a colleague to get some feedback on what works well and anything to change. *Remember practice makes better and practice makes permanent.*

_____

_____

_____

_____

17

"Minding Your APQs"

RON BEGAN THE next meeting with "Can you spot a fake bill? "Do you know what a counterfeited C-note—a $100 bill— looks like?

"Can you detect their fakeness traits, such as the inauthentic paper on which they are printed? After all, you can't go to Staples or Office Depot and buy that cotton-fiber paper.

"How about the lack of raised print? The sloppy engraving? The presidents who don't actually look like the presidents on the real bills? The rough, imperfectly engraved edges on the seal? The lack of security threads in the background?

"Do you know that $20 and $100 bills are the ones most commonly counterfeited in the United States? Watch for them!

"Yes, fake money sends you a lot of clues that the bills are not authentic. And the US treasury—as well as the treasuries of Canada, Mexico, and other countries—develops new and improved anticounterfeiting measures on an ongoing basis.

"When you examine a fake bill closely, it asks you questions that you can't answer. In that case, you know that it's a fake.

"But what about the inauthentic presenter, executive, teacher, or salesperson? Well, you can be very certain that your audience will spot all of the clues. And this is why I always say you can't fake it to make it! I spot a phony a mile away.

"Do you know *why* you are really there?

"Do you have a significant, meaningful, clear message?

"Are you fully prepared?

"Are you dressed for the audience you have authentically chosen to be in front of?

"The reality of today's business and professional world is that no one will take you seriously—or be convinced or 'sold' by your presentation—if you aren't authentic. That's why in all these sessions, we've emphasized authenticity.

"Today, we're going to discuss something known as APQs, or 'authentic presence qualities.' This is more about the *your presence* part of The Authenticity Code™. These are the traits that separate average people from extraordinary people. They are all key components of authenticity. If you turn to pages 11 and 12 in your day-one packet of handouts, you will see exactly what they are. You will also notice that there are blank spaces after each quality, so I encourage you to add your own thoughts.

"Dr. Sharon Lamm-Hartman, the CEO of Inside-Out Learning, researched key qualities that, if demonstrated, contribute to the expression of authentic presence. The basic qualities are warmth, thoughtfulness, openness, sincerity, integrity, clarity, passion, confidence, polish and presentation, inspiration, trustworthiness, and respect. If you've been counting, there are 12 of them. And they are all important.

"The next two pages in your packet will give you specifics on how you can demonstrate these authentic presence qualities.

"What I'd like you to do right now is spend about ten minutes to read and contemplate the items on the list. Then I'd like you to consider your competitor for the promotion. Josh, what two authentic presence qualities do you believe Rachel exhibits? And, Rachel, what qualities do you think Josh exemplifies? I'll ask for your thoughts after you've had time to think and jot down some notes."

Ron sat down next to Victoria, and Josh and Rachel closely studied the list of APQ qualities.

**APQ DEFINITIONS, AND EXAMPLES FOR
HOW TO DEMONSTRATE EACH:**

Clarity: The ability to communicate your message in an intuitively clear and compelling way.

1. Using the formula for presentation success

2. Stating your bottom line up front—a good Executive Summary

3. _____

4. _____

5. _____

Confidence: The air of assurance that communicates to others you have the required strength and resolve.

1. Believing in yourself

2. Being prepared to address even the most difficult questions

3. _____

4. _____

5. _____

Inspiration: The ability to passionately communicate the vision and mission of the organization, establish the inspirational culture of your organization, and breathe life into others.

1. Motivating a stalled team to move forward

2. Believing your people can achieve the mission, and helping them believe they can

3. _____

4. _____

5. _____

Integrity: The demonstration of alignment in your beliefs, words, and actions through the willingness to constructively share your point of view and follow through on your commitments.

1. Following through on your commitments or renegotiating

2. Living your values and ethical standards

3. _____

4. _____

5. _____

Openness: The willingness to consider another's point of view, without prejudging.

1. Being inclusive and listening to another's point of view

2. Considering all options for the best possible outcome and not just your way

3. _____

4. _____

5. _____

Passion: The expression of commitment, motivation, and drive that shows people you really believe in what you do.

1. Communicating in an enthusiastic tone

2. Getting the project done with a positive attitude

3. _____

4. _____

5. _____

Polish and Presentation: The look of sophistication that conveys a background of education and experience.

1. Greeting clients with a firm handshake and positive eye contact
2. Dressing appropriately for the event and audience
3. Adjusting to others' communication style while not losing your own authenticity
4. _____
5. _____

Respect: The quality of valuing the thoughts and opinions of others and openly considering these as viable options and opportunities.

1. Maintaining good eye contact when speaking
2. Acknowledging that diverse opinions and experiences have value
3. _____
4. _____
5. _____

Sincerity: The quality of believing in and meaning what you say.

1. Walking your talk; living by example
2. Not believing or saying something just to be accepted
3. _____
4. _____
5. _____

Thoughtfulness: The projection of thinking or having thought through something before responding.

1. Reconsidering a position after hearing a colleague's stance
2. Calming down before responding when you're offended
3. _____
4. _____
5. _____

Trustworthiness: The quality of modeling true positive character traits and top-level competence in your profession.

1. Repeatedly performing at a high quality

2. Following through on your commitments

3. _____

4. _____

5. _____

Warmth: The quality of being accessible to others and of being interested in them.

1. Acknowledging someone for a job well done

2. Learning and speaking about what you know is special to someone

3. Smiling

4. _____

5. _____

When adequate time had passed to complete the exercise, Victoria got to her feet and handed Rachel and Josh the APQ "Other" assessment survey. "If you've been struggling with your assessment at all, this form will help you evaluate each other on how well you demonstrate each of the APQs. Please take a few minutes to complete it on one another, and after this session, I encourage you to give it to at least two other colleagues and ask them to complete it on you. This will help you identify your two strongest and weakest APQs."

RATE AUTHENTIC PRESENCE QUALITIES (APQS)—"OTHER"

Ask three or more people to rate you to help you determine your
APO strengths and blind spots.

Instructions. Please fill out this assessment for:

_____

How well does this person demonstrate each APQ? Rate this individual on
a scale from 1 to 5 (1–Needs Improvement; 3–Average; 5–Amazing). Once complete,
fill in the blanks below to identify the two lowest- and two highest-rated APQs.

		Needs Improvement				Amazing
Clarity	The ability to communicate your message in an intuitively clear and compelling way.	1	2	3	4	5
Confidence	The air of assurance, such that others know you have the required strength and resolve.	1	2	3	4	5
Inspiration	Feeling passionately about the vision and mission of the organization. The ability to communicate that passion, purpose, and meaning establishes the inspirational culture of the organization. Breathing life into others.	1	2	3	4	5
Integrity	Your beliefs, works, and actions are aligned and demonstrated through the willingness and skills to constructively share your point of view and follow through on your commitments.	1	2	3	4	5
Openness	No prejudging; the willingness to consider another's point of view.	1	2	3	4	5
Passion	The expression of commitment, motivation, and drive that shows people you really believe in what you do.	1	2	3	4	5

		Needs Improvement				Amazing
Polish and Presentation	The look of sophistication, conveying a background of education and experience.	1	2	3	4	5
Respect	Values the thoughts and opinions of others and openly considers these as viable options and opportunities.	1	2	3	4	5
Sincerity	The conviction of believing in and meaning what you say.	1	2	3	4	5
Thoughtfulness	The projection of thinking or having thought through something before responding.	1	2	3	4	5
Trustworthiness	Models true positive character qualities and top-level competence of their profession.	1	2	3	4	5
Warmth	The willingness to being accessible to others and of being interested in them.	1	2	3	4	5

Lowest-Rated APQs: _____ / _____

Highest-Rated APQs: _____ / _____

When a reasonable amount of time had passed, Ron asked Josh to go first.

"Well, I'm not just saying this, but I think that Rachel has so many authentic qualities that it's not easy to narrow it down to two."

"Thank you, Josh," Rachel responded, feeling increasingly confident. "But would you please try?"

Josh paused as he thought a bit more. "I personally think that Rachel excels in three areas: Passion, Confidence, and Respect."

Ron wanted to know more: "Can you explain those points in greater detail?"

"Okay, I'll try my best. By Passion, I mean that Rachel really wants this promotion, and she is really passionate about her work and her volunteer work. By Confidence, I mean that she believes she is truly the ideal candidate, and she always seems willing, if not eager, to address the most difficult questions. And by Respect, I think that Rachel has good eye contact, and she respects my opinions and experiences. Even though—and I admit this—I can sometimes be the butt of that HORSE we've been talking about, she respects me enough to accept my quirks."

Rachel boldly responded, "Thank you, Mr. Quirk!"

Both Ron and Victoria (and even Josh) just about lost their composure here.

Ron immediately jumped in. "Okay, Rachel. Your turn. Don't forget to be passionate, confident, and respectful!"

"Got it," she replied, half laughing.

"Josh, if there were categories for 'Humor,' or even 'Sarcasm,' you'd be the clear winner! Don't get me wrong . . . I really like that about you. I find it refreshing, but not at all 'corporate.' If I'm being honest, while it is authentic, it just doesn't seem to fit the culture of World Wide Synergistics. It seems to me much like wearing a clown suit to a funeral. Inappropriate.

"But before you give up on me, I *do* think you have great authentic presence qualities. First, you are Trustworthy. Anytime you've promised me new technical product information for me to use in our social media campaigns, you deliver on time. And it's always accurate to the tiniest detail. Kind of nerdy, actually, but I appreciate it!

"Your second great APQ is Clarity. You don't miss *anything*, Josh! Your emails and memos to me are *super clear and to the point*. If I miss some teeny point you are making, I'm positive it's my fault.

"Finally, I would add Sincerity. To me, that means, 'What we see is what we get.' Maybe that's honesty. Maybe it's your 'no baloney' approach to life. Maybe it's because you really believe an old rock from your backyard in Brooklyn really *is* a billion-year-old dinosaur egg. Whatever it is, you *do* come off as sincere."

"Thank you, Rachel! I sincerely mean that, from the bottom of my heart."

Ron chimed in, "Lest you think we are done for the day, I have one more assignment for you. I want you to spend the next five minutes reviewing the list of APQs again. But this time, evaluate yourself. What do you believe your own APQs really are? This is your self-evaluation. Your personal assessment. The self-assessment APQ form is the next page in your packet of handouts. This time, I want to hear your two lowest-rated APQs, which are the two that you most want to work on." After this meeting, I can email you both an interactive PDF of the APQ self-assessment and APQ other assessment form so you can use them again. If you prefer, you can go to insideoutlearning.com/mobileapps/, and download three steps of IOL's Authenticity Code™ mobile app which includes the self APQ assessment and it allows you to communicate with a community of peers. But for now please use your handout to complete the self assessment."

RATE YOUR AUTHENTIC PRESENCE QUALITIES (APQS)—"SELF"

How well do you demonstrate each APQ?

Instructions. Rate yourself on a scale from 1 to 5
(1 = Needs Improvement, 3 = OK, 5 = Amazing)

Once complete, fill in the blanks below to identify your two
lowest-rated APQ's and your two highest.

		Needs Improvement				Amazing
Clarity	The ability to communicate your message in an intuitively clear and compelling way.	1	2	3	4	5
Confidence	The air of assurance, such that others know you have the required strength and resolve.	1	2	3	4	5
Inspiration	Feeling passionately about the vision and mission of the organization. The ability to communicate that passion, purpose, and meaning establishes the inspirational culture of the organization. Breathing life into others.	1	2	3	4	5
Integrity	Your beliefs, works, and actions are aligned and demonstrated through the willingness and skills to constructively share your point of view and follow through on your commitments.	1	2	3	4	5
Openness	No prejudging; the willingness to consider another's point of view.	1	2	3	4	5
Passion	The expression of commitment, motivation, and drive that shows people you really believe in what you do.	1	2	3	4	5
Polish and Presentation	The look of sophistication, conveying a background of education and experience.	1	2	3	4	5

		Needs Improvement				Amazing
Respect	Values the thoughts and opinions of others and openly considers these as viable options and opportunities.	○ 1	○ 2	○ 3	○ 4	○ 5
Sincerity	The conviction of believing in and meaning what you say.	○ 1	○ 2	○ 3	○ 4	○ 5
Thoughtfulness	The projection of thinking or having thought through something before responding.	○ 1	○ 2	○ 3	○ 4	○ 5
Trustworthiness	Models true positive character qualities and top-level competence in your profession.	○ 1	○ 2	○ 3	○ 4	○ 5
Warmth	The willingness to being accessible to others and of being interested in them.	○ 1	○ 2	○ 3	○ 4	○ 5

Lowest-Rated APQs: _____ / _____

Highest-Rated APQs: _____ / _____

They both dug in immediately. Ron loved their open and eager attitude!

Josh raised his hand. "Okay, I'm finished."

Rachel quickly responded, "I am, too. I need to work on Clarity—such as shortening my presentations and following the formula for presentation success. I also need to work on Confidence—while others believe in me, I sometimes have a hard time believing in myself, which is why I tend to have perfectionism tendencies."

"Great insights, Rachel! Josh, how about you?" Ron asked.

"Okay. I rated myself low on Polish and Presentation. As Rachel said earlier, 'What you see is what you get.' I am not trying to fake my way through anything. The real reason I don't shine my shoes like an army private is that I don't have time for what I consider to be 'insignificant nonsense.' The world is confronting too many important issues, and I want to help solve them. Sorry, Ron. I don't feel I would be authentic in dressing for this culture, so I need to work on other ways I can authentically demonstrate Polish and Presentation, like with my less-cluttered slides.

"Second, I believe I need to work on demonstrating Respect. Ron, I respect you for what you have worked so hard to teach both of us. Rachel, I respect you for what you do to help those who have serious illnesses. Even though I have never had a close friend or relative who battled cancer, I admire and respect your devotion to the ... the ... whatever you said."

"Leukemia and Lymphoma Society," Rachel said. "And lucky you, not having anyone in your world who faces such an awful battle!"

"I know. I am grateful for that," Josh agreed. "However, the reason I feel I need to work on demonstrating Respect is—like you said, Rachel—I tend to be sarcastic, and that can make people think I don't respect them. I'm making a commitment to you both to work on respecting others' opinions and to work on dropping the sarcasm."

At this point, Ron took control of the focus and direction of the meeting. "You might be asking, 'Why do I need to develop my APQs?' It is because Inside-Out Learning believes authentic presence accounts for at least 26 percent of what it takes to get promoted, make a sale, or get a yes in any presentation or communication you deliver. This means that if you are competing with someone else for a job or to close a deal, the person with the most authentic presence will prevail."

Ron continued: "I need to inform both of you that this is the wrap-up of our sessions. Next week is the third battle round. Remember, preparation is essential. Please practice everything you've learned, and aim for being better than your past best. And most of all, show up demonstrating the APQs that you're strongest in and that you are working on."

Josh raised his hand. "I have a question. It may be my last one. Why has it required so many meetings to make your decision? This seems to me to be such a simple, basic decision. I'm sure that both Rachel and I could handle the promotion."

"I'm sure you both could. But this is all about the future. The future of this company. Your future careers . . . and your long-term success. And even my future as a leader. If I were to mess this up, we would all be messed up. Our company is like a huge puzzle. One missing piece, one piece out of place, and the entire puzzle is a disaster. It simply doesn't work. It doesn't all fit together. So that is the underlying reason why authenticity is so important."

TAKE A MOMENT . . .

1. Think about a coworker you admire and with whom you work closely. What APQs do you think they exhibit? Consider sharing your thoughts with that individual.

_____

_____

_____

_____

2. Now think about yourself for a few minutes. You can complete the self-assessment on pages 133–134. What APQs do you believe you most effectively demonstrate? And what two APQs do you most need to develop?

_____

_____

_____

_____

3. Download three free mobile APP steps at insideoutlearning.com/ mobileapps/ to further develop the "your presence" part of the Authenticity Code™. Complete the three steps that include an interactive APQ self-assessment form and fun videos that allow you to assess APQ's in different professional scenarios. The third step helps you to plan how to develop your APQ's. Remember, you can also ask others to give you feedback on the APQ's they believe you are strongest in and those you could develop in. Unless we know how others view us, we can't authentically choose whether we want to work on our growth and development.

_____

_____

_____

_____

18

Surprise, Surprise!

PRESENTATION DAY—THE SECOND and final "battle round"—arrived before Josh and Rachel felt they were thoroughly prepared. While the two of them did individual preparation, they approached their preparation in different ways. Rachel spent more time on the science of success—improving her visuals, following the formula for presentation success, and practicing by video recording herself twice and reviewing the videos. She even asked her best friend to give her feedback on the videos. Josh poured his heart and soul into crafting his Authentic Brand Statement by answering the ten questions Ron had provided. He focused more on the art of success, because he realized that he was the presentation. He spent his preparation getting more in touch with who he truly was.

Being the perfectionist she was, Rachel wished she had even more time to practice and record herself at least one more time. Josh felt really confident in what he was presenting but became a bit concerned about how being totally authentic would impact his career.

They both showed up to the conference room. Ron was dressed in a full suit and tie, and Victoria was dressed in a beautiful navy-blue business suit with a magenta silk blouse. The feeling as they walked into the room was way more formal than any of their previous sessions. Rachel and Josh both realized this was it; this was the final session where they would learn who got the job. Following what was apparently established protocol, Rachel presented first.

Victoria and especially Ron were immediately impressed by her professional appearance. Rachel was dressed in an executive pantsuit with a red blazer (her power color) and black pants. She wore a white blouse that her sorority sister who survived cancer had given her. She also wore her favorite black pumps and gold long necklace.

She had gotten into the conference room early to test that her clicker worked and that her slides were all showing the way they should. When Victoria and Ron looked at Rachel, they realized she was indeed becoming the authentic executive she was born to be. It was clear that she really wanted this promotion.

Even Josh noticed as she strode up to the podium. "Looking great, Rachel! Show us how it's done," he encouraged softly.

Rachel then again made a solid case as to why she should get the promotion. She not only looked the part; she also spoke with confidence and clarity.

She delivered her carefully crafted Authentic Brand Statement as her attention-getting opening: "I am the associate director of Sales at World Wide Synergistics, who transforms the Sales Department into the number-one sales team in the industry. I inspire the team to genuinely care about our customers' needs, and we win industry awards for our customer service. I do this by demonstrating my greatest gifts of nurturing, compassion, and commitment to exceptional results."

She then shared her Executive Summary by stating that her purpose was to demonstrate why she was the best candidate for the job. Her value proposition was that she would grow sales revenue by 50 percent while taking the Sales Department to the number-one sales team in the industry. She completed her Executive Summary with a bold ask and looked directly in Ron's eyes and said, "My desired outcome is that you, Ron, choose me as the final candidate for the associate director of Sales position."

She went on to show her agenda, which was her past experience, present results, and future plan if selected for the job. Her HORSE was alive and well. Her points were clear, and her visuals were spot-on! With each agenda point, Rachel highlighted the point, clearly said "okay, so what," provided relevant information, and eased into the next point or to her close. She never needed to summarize each point because the presentation was short. She followed Ron's guidance with her slides and never used less than 21-point Arial font. She used Appear animation to bring on bullets one by one so she was in control of what her audience was seeing.

Ron, Victoria, and Josh were blown away by what Rachel did to Finish Strong. She started with a black blank slide so all eyes were completely focused on her, and she first repeated her ask by making direct eye contact with Ron and saying, "Ron, I hope I have proven to you that I am the best candidate for this position and that in the end you award me the associate director of Sales position." She continued, "I want to thank you all for helping me crack The Authenticity Code™. I never realized that my presence plus my audience plus my presentation was the key to my success. You helped me uncover things about myself that were unconscious until the past few weeks. My perfectionism covered up a deep insecurity that others may find out I am not as good as I appear to be. While others saw me as confident, I never felt confident inside. I also did not realize how passionate I was about sales until taking this journey with you all.

"Ron, Victoria, and Josh, your belief in me and my abilities, the time you freely gave to help me better myself, and the tools, experiences, and dress tips you shared with me helped me finally believe in myself. I can honestly say as I stand before you today that I am more confident than I ever have been in myself and my abilities. While I am not perfect, I have grown more in a few weeks than I have in my 30 years of life. So not only have you helped me master the science of success with so many awesome Authenticity Code™ formulas, tools, guidelines, and exercises, but you also helped me learn the art of success. For now in this very moment that I share with you"—she clicked the remote to her final slide—"I know in all my being that I *am the presentation.*" Centered in the middle of a black slide in white letters were simply the words "I am the presentation!"

Ron and Victoria looked at each other with tears in their eyes. Josh felt chills as Rachel uttered her final words. Even Rachel had tears in her eyes as she said, "I am the presentation!" Ron had to wipe his cheek. Seeing Rachel in her true authenticity made him feel as if he was living his authentic brand of mentoring his protégés.

On top of all that, she nailed the time. She stepped away from the front of the room at exactly 14 minutes and 58 seconds—just under the 15 minutes she had been allotted. As Rachel took her seat, she couldn't mistake the broad grins on the faces of both Ron and Victoria. It was like their personal versions of high fives.

In fact, Josh led the applause.

Then Ron noted, "Josh, you're fortunate that you had the opportunity to observe Rachel in action. There is no better way to learn what you're up against."

Josh nodded, nervous.

"You ready, buddy?" Ron asked with an affirming tone.

"As ready as I will ever be," Josh replied.

"Remember," Victoria coached from the sidelines, "The Authenticity Code™ is Your Presence + Your Audience + Your Presentation = Your Success."

"Got it," Josh mumbled as he hesitantly and haltingly made his way to the front of the room, but instead of stepping up to the lectern, he pushed it away so he could not hide behind it.

He wiped visible sweat from his forehead and began.

"First of all, I need to thank Ron for his confidence in me. And I want to thank both Ron and Dr. Reynolds for their coaching and for their teachings about authenticity.

"I also want to thank my colleague Rachel for demonstrating authenticity to me throughout this entire selection process, as well as in the presentation she just finished. Rachel, I believe that you truly deserve every opportunity that ever comes your way."

Rachel looked down at her feet, as if embarrassed. "Thank you, Josh," she said kindly.

"Now it's my turn," Josh continued. "By that, I mean it's not just my turn to present, but it's my turn to become authentic."

Puzzled looks crossed everyone's faces.

With that, Josh unbuttoned his seldom-worn suit jacket and flung it into the empty chair on the back side of the podium. Next, he nearly ripped off his color-coordinated tie and tossed that on top of his jacket. What remained was a standard white polo shirt tucked into khaki casual pants with a brown belt and his new favorite pair of sneakers.

"Don't worry, folks!" he said. "Yes, this was part of my 'attention-getting opening,' but that is as far as I will go! And at least it is a step up from my first presentation. The only reason I wore khaki pants was out of respect for you Ron, because I know you care about that stuff. I guess they call this business casual, maybe with the exception of my sneakers, which still feel authentic to me."

Chuckles followed.

"But my point in doing that is very simple. A suit and tie are not a part of the 'Authentic Joshua Armstrong.' You know me. I am most comfortable in faded blue jeans, T-shirts or sweatshirts, a Vanderbilt baseball cap, and scuffed-up sneakers. I'm not cut out to impress C-suite executives . . . neither here nor in the offices of our clients.

"Bottom line up front, I do not want this promotion. I'm not the right guy. This promotion rightfully belongs to Rachel Hannigan. I hope you give it to her. She deserves it."

Then Josh returned to his seat, leaving everyone stunned.

Ron jumped to his feet. "Wait a minute! You ran way short. You have several minutes remaining."

Josh replied, "I don't need those minutes."

"Okay, fair enough. But who is the Authentic Joshua Armstrong? Can you please tell us that?"

With that, Josh returned to the front of the room. "Okay. I did what you recommended, Ron, and I took Inside Out Learning's style recognition assessment. I'm almost tied between a point person and a planner person: I think logically, and I communicate clearly and concisely. In fact, Rachel observed that clarity is one of my APQ strengths. I tend to keep things short, brief, and to the point. Yet I always want to justify and prove what I and others think. I want all the facts before making a decision, and I don't like surprises. I also love to spend creative time alone inventing new ideas that can be patented. I really don't care about being part of a sales department.

"But in terms of my personal goals and achievements, here is what I believe is my Authentic Brand Statement:

'I am the best engineer in any industry, and, at last count, I own 13 patents . . . with several more under review. My inventions keep our nation and our allies safe by preventing a potential war in space and by providing better, more timely detailed analyses of various global threats, including hurricanes, typhoons, floods, volcanic eruptions, and crop failures. The satellite images I have been able to capture will save countless lives for untold decades. I achieve these things by utilizing my greatest gifts of analytical and innovative thinking. The most important thing I want to know when I retire is that our planet will still be here and that life is supported to the best of our knowledge and abilities.'"

Rachel couldn't contain herself. "Wow! And here, all this time, I thought you were just a quiet, shy geek who wrote great product manuals and marketing materials!"

It was a bold observation on her part, but still, everyone laughed. Rachel was relieved.

Ron broke the ensuing silence. "Josh, I really appreciate your honesty. After all, that really is important to authenticity. This is why you can't fake it to make it. Faking it is never authentic."

"Thank you, Ron."

"But my question is, Do you believe there is some other role for you in our company?"

"Uh, I'm really not sure," Josh admitted.

"May I suggest something based on watching you and listening to what you said?"

"Of course." Josh nodded, truly interested.

"Have you ever heard of International Space Solutions, Inc.?"

"I sure have! ISSI is one of the new leaders in unmanned space technology, soon to venture into manned missions."

"Exactly," Ron agreed. "In fact, the founder and CEO of ISSI is a former air force buddy of mine, General Al Scinto. He's looking for talented innovators. I could put you in touch with him if you would be interested."

"WOULD I EVER!" Josh was now on the edge of his seat, soaking up every word.

"One thing you should know, though. Even though Al is retired military, we are not similar at all. Al is not a stickler for protocol. His dress code is 'anything goes.' And he encourages his engineers to work from home, to get away from the politics of the workplace in order to engage in unfettered creativity. He is all about solutions!"

"Works for me. You obviously know I'm not a suit-and-tie guy anyway."

"That's why I thought you might be a good fit. I'll give you his contact information. He prefers email, and he is a planner type guy like you but also appreciates a good BLUF (also like you). So follow your gut and, as you say, 'cut to the chase.'"

"Got it. Thanks, Ron!"

"You're welcome, Josh."

"No, Ron. Really. I mean thank you for caring. Thank you for your personal involvement. Thank you for teaching Rachel and me about the significance of The Authenticity Code™. I would have never gotten in touch with who I truly am and wouldn't have stopped being a fake without this valuable training. You're a life changer, no doubt about it!"

TAKE A MOMENT . . .

1. What did Rachel do right?

_____

_____

_____

_____

2. What did Josh do right?

_____

_____

_____

_____

3. In what ways were they both authentic?

_____

_____

_____

_____

4. In what ways are you being authentic?

_____

_____

_____

_____

5. In what ways might you be faking it to make it, and how do you plan to use the Authenticity Code™ to help you step into more of your authentic self?

_____

_____

_____

_____

Epilogue
A Final Word from the Author

BECAUSE I AM the creator of APPS—and sometimes the lead presenter as well—I have had the opportunity, over the years, to meet and work with many people who remind me of Ron, Victoria, Rachel, and Josh. They may also suggest people with whom you have worked in the past.

Because I also understand the events and stories surrounding their illustrious careers, I feel that I also have the right to tell you (or maybe simply "imagine") how their lives continued to evolve.

You have likely determined that, in the "almost perfect world" of World Wide Synergistics, Rachel was awarded the promotion to the position of Ron's associate director of Sales. Not only did Rachel become *authentic*, but so did Josh, her competitor for the promotion. He willingly backed off—only partly in order to let her achieve what she wanted—and moved on himself.

Don't feel a lot of sympathy for Josh, though. He got what he wanted, too. He was empowered to create, invent all sorts of new stuff, and wear his favorite sneakers to work—*when* he actually went to work in an office.

Mostly, though, he worked at home, sometimes 18 hours a day, inventing a better, safer world. Unlike many companies in these somewhat greedy times, his new employer—International Space Solutions, Inc. (ISSI)—permitted Josh to retain the rights to all of his patented inventions. And there were *lots* of those. So many, in fact, that they are flying above your head right now. *Way* above. Seriously! (Josh was eventually nominated for the Nobel Prize in Physics. He didn't win, but he didn't care. Being authentic was what really mattered to him. That, and his adopted shelter dog, Explorer, aptly named after the first satellite put into orbit by the United States back in 1958.)

Victoria had loved Human Resources since she assembled the brilliant team that she led in the creation of her award-winning high school yearbook. She did the same exact thing at Northwestern University in Illinois. "Building great teams is what I want to do with my life," she declared as she pursued her degrees in psychology and human resource management. The truth is, Victoria was the one who hired Ron, rescuing him from a life of early retirement as an ex-military guy.

Just kidding. Ron didn't do badly for himself, as you have probably guessed. I *love* happy endings. And Ron gets one, too!

Ron's Authentic Brand Statement said this:

"I am the CEO of World Wide Synergistics, who seeks out and hires the most competent, skilled, innovative individuals I can identify for every position that needs to be filled, and I inspire and empower them to succeed beyond their greatest expectations. I foster positive attitudes toward our company and model healthy workplace relationships. I give this by encouraging, supporting, and motivating people to exceed what they thought was possible."

So, did Ron Burk ever become the CEO of World Wide Synergistics? Sadly no. Does that mean that Ron failed the "authenticity test"? Joyously, also, NO!

Ron, with his firmly ingrained advancement-driven military mentality, was given an opportunity that was even better than being the CEO of World Wide Synergistics. He left the company to join the team of his friend, General Al Scinto, at ISSI. Al knew Ron's greatest gifts and asked him to become his partner and co-lead ISSI. Al focused on the technical and financial side of the business, and Ron was involved with the people, the culture, and the development side. Together they made an outstanding team that took ISSI to new heights as a major player in the "keeping space safe" industry.

Ron partly made this choice because ISSI was an exciting new venture in an exciting new field, and he could focus on "being" his Authentic Brand Statement.

Part of the reason was that it gave him the opportunity to share The Authenticity Code™ with more people. He bought this book for everyone at ISSI and brought Inside-Out Learning in to deliver their Authenticity Code™ programs for all ISSI professionals and leaders. But *most* of the reason was that he'd have the opportunity to work at the same company with his brilliant protégé Joshua Armstrong—and wear his favorite sneakers to work. After years of dressing more formal for work, Ron really enjoyed a more casual work environment.

Each of the characters ended up living their Authentic Brand Statements. They took the risk to do so. Sometimes it does not look exactly as you think it will, as in Ron's case: Instead of being CEO of World Wide Synergistics, he became a partner at ISSI, doing something better than he ever imagined.

What do you need to do to crack The Authenticity Code™ in your life?

What do you need to become the real you?

Think about it because you can't fake it to make it!

Important P.S.'s:

THE PRIMARY GOALS of this book—and, in fact, all materials from Inside-Out Learning, Inc.—are to empower you with the skills and tools you need to face *any* audience in any setting, and help you to do the following:

- Connect
- Convey
- Convince
- Complete

That last point is vital to any presenter, because it means that you are bold enough to "go for the sale." You are confident enough to ask for the desired action . . . the decision.

IMPORTANT LEADERSHIP PRESENCE FACTS

A survey of 268 senior executives revealed "Executive Presence counts for at least 26 percent of what it takes to get promoted."[3]

---

3   Center for Talent Innovation.

However, that is by far the lowest number I have ever heard. The highest estimates are closer to 80–90 percent, with the remainder made up of your specific skill set. No matter which number you believe, authentic presence is still an important factor in how successful you will be as a leader and in your professional career. Think about it if you are competing for a job with someone who has similar accomplishments and skills; the only thing that will differentiate you is your leadership presence. The job will go to the most authentic person.

OUR DEFINITION OF AUTHENTIC PRESENCE

Authentic presence is "how you affect others by the impression you make with your physical presence, your demeanor, your presentation of thoughts, and the general mode of conversation you have with others."

OUR DEFINITION OF AUTHENTICITY

Your most powerful way of adding value by expressing your unique gifts and talents for your chosen audience.

Services Offered/Contact Us

FREE AUTHENTICITY CODE™ SERVICES

Inside-Out Learning is here to support you in becoming authentic and in practicing the Authenticity Code™, with many free services, because it is our mission to help as many professionals and leaders as possible be who they came here to be and do what they came here to do. We hope you take advantage of our free and paid services.

FREE LINKEDIN COMMUNITY OF PRACTICE FOR OUR READERS

My company Inside-Out Learning is here to support you in continuing to become authentic and in practicing The Authenticity Code™. Please join our free Community of Practice at linkedin.com/groups/13841506/, where we post weekly best practices, tools, and research to help you on your Authenticity Code™ journey. We also help you dialogue with others who are also on this journey so you have the support you need to grow.

Having a like-minded supportive community is key to your success.

THREE-STEP FREE AUTHENTICITY CODE™ APP DEMO

Simply download three free steps to level up the "your presence" part of the Authenticity Code™ (insideoutlearning.com/mobileapps/). Each step takes 15 minutes to complete and will help you reinforce what you learned about the "your presence" part of the Authenticity Code™ in this book. You will watch videos, practice tools, and communicate with others who are completing the app at the same time. You can download directly to your cell phone or iPad and complete these steps at your leisure or at convenient times during your real work day. If you love the app and want the remaining 12 steps, simply go to the same link to purchase our app (insideoutlearning.com/mobileapps/) and enter promo code TACAPPS for a 10 percent discount.

FREE STYLE RECOGNITION ASSESSMENT

In gratitude for you purchasing this book, you receive one free style recognition assessment so you can see which of the four styles is your main personality preference—a people person, point person, party person, or planner person. Simply go to this link to download the assessment: insideoutlearning.com/style/.

PAID AUTHENTICITY CODE™ SERVICES

If you are really serious about cracking The Authenticity Code™ to achieve your desired level of career and business success, promise me you will invest in yourself as well as your company or organization. Practice makes permanent. In each of our paid programs, you will work on an actual presentation that you will give in the future, and you will master The Authenticity Code™ and delivering that presentation. This is how our clients have won billions of dollars in sales, received promotions (50 to 80 percent of participants who go through our three- to five-day programs are promoted within one year of completing our program), and developed critical professional and leadership skills. We would love to continue to support you in one or more of the following ways.

15-STEP AUTHENTICITY CODE™ APP

If you love the free three-step app on the "your presence" part of the

Authenticity Code™ and want the remaining 12 steps, simply go to the same link to purchase our app (insideoutlearning.com/mobileapps/) and enter promo code TACAPPS for a 10 percent discount. This app is state of the art technology that reminds you to do your daily 15-minute action steps to develop five key Authenticity Code™ habits. There are steps for practicing and developing the entire Authenticity Code™—Your Presence + Your Audience + Your Presentation = Your Success. This helps you crack the code to become who you came here to be and do what you came here to do. You can participate in a peer community of learners who are also doing the app at the same time. You can take your time in completing the steps and enjoy the journey. You will develop an actual presentation you will use in the future, as well as practice presence and audience tools you learned in this book.

VIRTUAL FACILITATOR-LED PUBLIC AUTHENTICITY CODE™ PROGRAMS

We offer several options for virtual facilitator-led programs, everything from watching pre-recorded videos to being part of live virtual facilitator led programs to adding on coaching sessions with an opportunity to be video recorded and receive peer and expert feedback, as well as a final video review with an Inside-Out Learning (IOL) expert. Please go to insideout-learning.com/tac/ to see the options to enroll in one of our public programs. Please enter VIRTUALAPPS as the code that will give you a 10 percent discount on any program you choose, to thank you for buying this book.

AUTHENTICITY CODE™ COACHING SESSIONS

We offer Authenticity Code™ individual coaching sessions in packages. You tell your IOL-certified coach which part of the code you want to delve more into—Your Presence + Your Audience + Your Presentation = Your Success. We focus where your interest lies, and can also help you develop high-stakes presentations that you need to deliver. Please go to insideoutlearning.com/coaching/ to learn more about our coaching packages, and enter COACHINGAPPS as the code to receive a 10 percent discount on any coaching packages.

AUTHENTICITY CODE™ SERVICES FOR COMPANIES & ORGANIZATIONS

We also offer digital, virtual, and in-person Authenticity Code™ programs for Fortune 500 and small to midsize companies, as well as universities and community organizations. Many of our clients buy our app for all of their employees, and then offer virtual training programs for professionals, emerging leaders, and managers, as well as in-person training programs for high-potential managers and executives. Our Authenticity Code™ programs have helped our clients earn billions of dollars in revenue, provided up to 80 percent promotion rates and 90 percent retention rates for our clients, and dramatically improved professional and leadership presence, presentation, and influence skills. We are happy to help you or your company or organization. Simply check out our website, insideoutlearning.com, or email me personally at drsharon@insideoutlearning.com. We would love to continue to support you, your company, and your organization.

We would also love to see you on our social media platforms and YouTube channel:

- Dr. Sharon Lamm-Hartman, Personal LinkedIn: linkedin.com/in/drsharonlammhartman/
- IOL LinkedIn: linkedin.com/company/insideoutlearning
- IOL Community of Practice: linkedin.com/groups/13841506/
- Twitter: twitter.com/IOL_inc
- Instagram: @Inside_out_learning
- Facebook: facebook.com/InsideOutLearninginc
- YouTube: youtube.com/channel/UCijY0JMtFrSJynAwC08XHrg

About the Author

DR. SHARON LAMM-HARTMAN is an award-winning global executive and presentation coach, leadership development consultant, speaker, writer, and educator. She is the CEO and founder of Inside-Out Learning, Inc., (IOL) specializing in leadership, team, and organization development. IOL is an active member of the global Women's President Organization, which only 3 percent of women-owned businesses meet the requirements to join. IOL is also a WBENC and WOSB certified company. IOL is recognized for its virtual learning program expertise, with hundreds of virtual learning programs and several learning APPS that can be directly downloaded to your cell phones.

With 25 years of global experience, Dr. Sharon has worked throughout the United States and Europe, as well as in Australia, Beijing, Hong Kong, Singapore, and Thailand, for clients such as Boeing, Virgin Orbit, VOX Space, Dexcom, Momentus, American Express, GE's Leadership Development Center, Exxon, E*TRADE, ARCO Chemical Company, Exxon Mobil Oil Corporation, Berlex Pharmaceuticals, Fannie Mae, Arizona Society of CPAs, Volvo Trucks Global, and WBENC. She has designed and delivered over 3,000 innovative programs, including many authentic presence and presentation skills programs. Dr. Sharon has coached and trained thousands of CEOs, executives, and entrepreneurs worldwide.

In addition to working in her private practice, consulting, and being on the global lecture circuit, Dr. Sharon has served with the Fresh Start

Women's Foundation and Arizona State University's Dean's Board of Excellence Mentoring Program. She was the cofounder and first director of Central Phoenix Women, a networking organization for women business leaders, and wrote a regular column for *Phoenix Woman Magazine*. She is also a speaker for WBENC WeTHRIVE programs.

Dr. Sharon holds a doctorate from Columbia University in leadership and organization development, a master's in industrial and labor relations from Cornell University, and two bachelor's degrees. She also trained as a life coach with world-renowned author and life coach teacher Dr. Martha Beck. Dr. Sharon is a certified executive and presentation coach and is certified in the Myers-Briggs Type Indicator.

She's been an adjunct professor of leadership at Columbia University, where she has taught leadership classes to doctorate-level students. She also worked as an adjunct faculty member at the Center for Creative Leadership, teaching courses on developing leadership talent.

Dr. Sharon has been quoted on her views of coaching in numerous publications, including Arianna Huffington's *Authority Magazine* and *Thrive Global*, *The New York Times*, *More* magazine, and *O, The Oprah Magazine*. She has been honored and received awards from the Center for Creative Leadership and the Academy of Human Resource Development for her work and research on personal transformation and leadership development.